BECOMING A MILLIONAIRE GOD'S WAY PART II

DR. C. THOMAS ANDERSON

Harrison House
Tulsa, OK

Copyright © 2014 Winword Publishing
Mesa, Arizona 85213

17 16 15 14   5 4 3 2 1

Published by: Harrison House Publishers
Tulsa, OK 74145
www.harrisonhouse.com

ISBN: 978-160683-980-5

TABLE OF CONTENTS

INTRODUCTION

"Go into all the world and preach the Gospel." These words are familiar to virtually every born–again believer. They come from Mark 16:15. Almost from the time that we meet Jesus, we are encouraged to share our faith with others. It is the Great Commission. We have a responsibility to spread the Gospel worldwide.

The problem is that few of us really understand what the Gospel is all about. Most Christians don't think of it in terms of much more than just getting people saved so they can go to heaven. Consequently, that is all that they preach. This produces a couple of problems in the life of the church today and in the fulfilling of the Great Commission.

First, people are born again and then struggle through life, barely surviving, always behind on bills, constantly sick, just getting by. Then they wonder why no one listens to the message they preach about God's love. Why would a God who loves make His people live that way? It doesn't make much sense to potential converts. So they remain potential.

Secondly, it is difficult for anyone to go into the world when they don't have enough money to live on and they're too sick to get out of bed. Preaching the Gospel requires resources and health, whether you are helping in your local church or going to the mission field. People in poverty don't preach very effectively.

Fortunately, this is not what the Gospel is. When Jesus used the word Gospel, He had in mind saving a lot more than just your soul. That was only the beginning. He set out to restore everything to man that was lost in the Garden of Eden. In fact, it is in the Garden that we see the first picture of God's plan for us.

The first time that we see God dealing with mankind, it says that He "blessed" them, man and woman (Genesis 1:28). The word blessed in the original Hebrew means to be highly favored, healthy, wealthy and joy-filled. It is in the picture of the Garden that we see just how much this related to their physical existence.

> The LORD God planted a garden eastward
> in Eden, and there He put the man whom He had
> formed. And out of the ground the LORD God
> made every tree grow that is pleasant to the sight
> and good for food. The tree of life was also in the
> midst of the garden, and the tree of the knowledge
> of good and evil (Genesis 2:8-9).

Man found life in the Garden. There was food to eat. There was beauty that was there for no other reason than because it was pleasing to the eye. There was security and protection. The Hebrew word for "garden" is *gan*. It specifically describes a place that was hedged in or fenced. It was a protected place.

The word "Eden" means joy, rapture, ornaments, finery, pleasure. It was literally a "garden of delight." It was a place of life. Adam and Eve had everything that they needed to be safe, happy, healthy, joy-filled and prosperous. They were blessed. This was their home, the place where they lived. They had it all. They had life.

This land becomes a picture of the family as Adam and Eve begin to have children. It is a place of relationships— Adam with Eve, both of them with their children, and Mankind with God. It is a prophetic picture of the New Testament *ekklesia*, the church, where the same relationships of giving and serving were to be the standard. It is from this home, the Paradise of Eden, that the Gospel is supposed to be preached.

From their home, the Garden, we are told that four rivers flow out. They are a picture of what the Gospel represents.

> *Now a river went out of Eden to water the garden, and from there it parted and became four riverheads. The name of the first is Pishon; it is the one which skirts the whole land of Havilah, where there is gold. And the gold of that land is good. Bdellium and the onyx stone are there. The name of the second river is Gihon; it is the one which goes around the whole land of Cush. The name of the third river is Hiddekel; it is the one*

which goes toward the east of Assyria. The fourth
river is the Euphrates (Genesis 2:10-14).

First of all, there is the symbolic picture of a river.
Throughout history, civilization has been connected to rivers. They are a vital source of water that humanity cannot
do without. In symbolism, the picture of a river, *nahar* in
Hebrew, combines two things. It is a life force or the breath
of the divine and it represents movement. A river pictures a
moving life force. Life flowed out of the Garden.

From the river in Eden, four rivers branched off. But
they represent more than just branches. The Hebrew indi-
cates that they are "riverheads," or starting points. The four
branches start from the life in the Garden.

The first river is the Pishon. It is a name that means
increase. It is described as flowing through the land of
Havilah where there is gold. Pishon represents prosperity.

The second river is the Gihon. The meaning of the
word is burst forth, or gushing forth. Gihon represents salvation. It is the bursting forth from the bondage of sin.

The third river is the Hiddekel, the Hebrew name for
the Tigris. It means rapid. It pictures the quick flight of
an arrow. It is described as flowing along the east side of
Asshur, a word that means successful. Hiddekel represents
success.

The fourth river is the Euphrates, the Greek form of the
Hebrew name Perat. It means fruitful. The Euphrates represents redeemed time, time that becomes fruitful instead
of wasted.

These four pictures represent the scope of the Gospel. It is a moving life force that proceeds from God through the family, or the church, and flows out to the world in the form of prosperity, salvation, success and redeemed time.

This explains why we can send missionaries to third world countries and see people get saved but they remain in poverty. Salvation is only one fourth of the Gospel. When we preach the Gospel to every creature, we are supposed to be doing much more than declaring salvation. We are also declaring success, prosperity and redeemed time.

I say all of this because some years ago, God spoke to me very clearly. As I related in *Becoming a Millionaire God's Way*, He said, "Many are teaching My people that they are to prosper, but no one is teaching them how." For many who read that, it seemed that my focus was on money, not the Gospel. But the truth is that you cannot preach the whole Gospel without teaching people to live in the abundance of God. It isn't about money. It's about being able to do all that God has called us to do without begging for the resources from other people. It is about being successful instead of downtrodden. It is about being efficient with our time instead of ineffective. It is about having the means to actually reach the world with the message of salvation. It is about having more than we need to accomplish things in this life. It is about having more success and more money than we actually need. The Gospel really is about having too much. Without having too much, it is impossible to fulfill the Great Commission.

Get the Right Attitude

When God spoke to me several years ago about teaching people how to prosper, He said that if I would teach what He told me, I would have one hundred millionaires in the church in three years. Over the next three years, I actually saw eighty-seven of them come to fruition. In four years, it went well over a hundred.

What is interesting about it, though, is how many of them are no longer around. Most are still with us, but for quite a few, their wealth took them in a different direction. They were tested by their success and found lacking. There is a danger inherent in wealth.

The Bible says we mut not despise small beginnings (Zechariah 4:10). It is important to start out in the process of gaining wealth by growing into the ability to handle it. Quick money is not good money. Easy money is not good money. Until you can handle it, money can destroy you. It is important to know in your own heart why you want too much.

So we have to understand some things about money before we have it. We have to understand our motives for wanting it in the first place.

For the sake of my brethren and companions, I will now say, "Peace be within you." Because of the house of the LORD our God I will seek your good (Psalm 122:8-9).

In this Psalm by David, the word "peace" is *shalom*

in Hebrew. It means wealth, goodness, health, prosperity, favor, happiness. Prosperity is another way of saying *shalom*. It is prosperity in every part of your life, which is what true peace is. Every time *shalom* is spoken, they are saying, "Prosperity to you." It is a wish for the person you are addressing to be prosperous, healthy, wealthy, peaceful and filled with joy. It includes all of those things.

Then, the next verse says that David sought good for the sake of the house of the Lord. "Good" is the Hebrew word *tov*. It has basically the same connotations as *shalom*. In fact, the New International Version translates it as "prosperity." For the sake of the house of the Lord, we are to seek prosperity. We are to seek the goodness of God, as it is shown in the covenant with Abraham. We seek too much health, too much prosperity, too much joy, too much wealth. But we are not to do it for selfish reasons. We are to seek it for the sake of the house of the Lord.

God wants us to have too much joy so that it flows over onto other people. If you don't have too much joy, it's difficult to give it away. He wants us to have too much wealth so that we can use it to serve Him and to serve others. It is imperative that we have this settled in our hearts. We seek too much wealth for the sake of building the Kingdom of God.

I am not saying that you should not enjoy wealth. When you have too much, it also means that you have everything that you need and everything that you want. It is a fascinating thing to see how it actually works. God's desire is for us to continually have too much so that we can use it for good purposes. But in the process, we get to enjoy it too.

God wants us to be a bright light. That means that we get to share. If you're sick or if you're just struggling to get by, if you've got oppression or depression, then nobody wants what you've got. But when you've got too much, you live in a nice home and drive a nice car, you've got peace and health and your finances are strong, then people will want to emulate you. They begin to wonder what causes your success. The key is to keep your priorities right.

Jesus said it early in His ministry:

> *But seek first the kingdom of God and His righteousness, and all these things shall be added to you* (Matthew 6:33).

In other words, if we keep the kingdom in front of us put kingdom principles first in everything we do, then the things that we desire will be added to us. Don't let things control you. You control things.

If we don't approach wealth with the right attitude, then the wealth becomes our master. When Adam first sinned, it says that the ground became cursed.

> *Cursed is the ground for your sake;*
> *In toil you shall eat of it*
> *All the days of your life* (Genesis 3:17).

It wasn't that God cursed the ground, but rather that the soil would not yield its fruit any longer without toil. In other words, the curse was, "You will toil for the soil."

God's ultimate plan, however, is to break the curse. The second Adam, Jesus Christ, came to set us back in the position where the soil toils for us, the same way that it did in the Garden before sin. Adam still had to work and tend the Garden even before the fall, so it wasn't just a matter of working or not working. Work is good. But before sin, the soil produced for him and he lived in the blessing. After sin, work lost its purpose and became more a matter of survival. It was a struggle instead of a joy.

Many of the passages of Scripture that have been cited by people who do not believe God wants prosperity for His people were actually written to deal with the motivation for seeking wealth. One of those passages is in Paul's letter to Timothy.

> *For the love of money is a root of all kinds of evil, for which some have strayed from the faith in their greediness, and pierced themselves through with many sorrows* (1 Timothy 6:10).

What had actually happened? They were in faith, but then something from their heart surfaced and steered them in another direction because of their greed. Their faith no longer was important to them, only the pursuit of money. Their things began to take control of them. The things their money could buy began to pull them away from the Word, away from church and away from growth in Christ. Money can do that.

But that doesn't make money bad. In fact, money is neither good nor bad. It is only a tool. It is not an object to be praised. It's not an object to be lifted above our knowledge of God. We have to pull those thoughts and strongholds down and subject them or submit them to the Word.

Notice that it does not say that money is the root of all evil. It is the love of money that is the problem. We're not supposed to love money. We're supposed to love God. When we keep that priority in order, God will take care of what money can do for us. It is a tool that is used for the work of the Kingdom of God.

Greed caused those who loved money to stray. The greed was stuck in their hearts and it produced many sorrows. God gave the solution just a few verses later. It wasn't to renounce wealth and become poor. It was to change their attitude and use the money wisely.

> *Command those who are rich in this present age not to be haughty, nor to trust in uncertain riches but in the living God, who gives us richly all things to enjoy* (1 Timothy 6:17).

To avoid straying from the faith because of greed, don't be haughty. Don't be prideful. Do not get caught up in things. Don't let things control you. Do not trust in riches.

There is nothing wrong with having great wealth as long as your trust is not in what's in the bank or in your stuff. Your trust needs to remain in God. In fact, it says specifically in that verse that God "gives us richly all things to enjoy."

Religion has used this verse for hundreds of years against the body of Christ to say that we shouldn't get rich. We should just stay poor. Of course, then they don't have to deal with greed. Unfortunately, greed is not limited to just rich people. Some of the greediest people around are also the poorest. It is a heart attitude. Stinginess will keep you poor.

There is one who scatters, yet increases more;
And there is one who withholds more than is right,
But it leads to poverty (Proverbs 11:24).

A fascinating characteristic of wealth is that it magnifies what is already in us. Many times, people say, "Well, I would give if I had a lot of money." If you say that, you are only fooling yourself. If you can't do something little, you'll never do something big. If you can't give at the level you're at now, you won't give at any level. It just won't happen. If you're stingy without money, you'll be stingy when you have it. In fact, you'll be even stingier than ever. You have to deal with the issues in you now or you'll never get to the next level.

This verse in Proverbs doesn't say that those who scattered are rich. It just says that they are willing to plant and to let go of what they have and that produces increase. Those who hang on to more than what is right will have poverty. Their wealth will not last. It will go right down the drain.

What is right? It is wisdom to have some money in the bank for whatever problems might come along. But when people begin to stockpile hundreds of thousands, millions or billions, there comes a point where it is greed and it is no longer right. God wants us to be rich for the right reasons. Otherwise, the wealth will fail us.

CHAPTER 1:

Capitalism in America

A merica is richer than any other nation on earth. We constitute only about a sixteenth of the worlds population, but we possess half of the world's wealth. The poorest person in America, the one living in a cardboard shack in a river bottom, has more wealth than two thirds of the people in the world. He has access to more food, better clothes and better health care.

The source of all this wealth is simple. It is capitalism. It is important that we recognize exactly what capitalism is. Webster's Dictionary defines it as: *"an economic system characterized by private ownership of goods by private decision, by an investment or investments that are determined by private decision rather than government or state controlled with prices, price of products, production and distribution of goods that are also determined by competition in a free market."*[1]

That is why America is called a land of opportunity. The entire economic system is designed to allow any individual to participate. And the result is a level of prosperity unknown to any other country in history. I will say here,

---

1 *Merriam-Webster Dictionary, S.V. "Capitalism"*

that capitalism is a biblical system. We will see this clearly as we study it.

For the past four hundred years in America, nearly anyone could own property. Right now, you can own a car. You can own land. You can own a business. By private decision, you can purchase things and have them as your own possessions. They are not owned by the government or by the church or by the nobility. You own them.

Do you realize that this situation is not the case in most nations? Just two hundred years ago in Europe, you didn't own land. A nobleman did. He gave you a plot of land to work and then taxed you until you stayed extremely poor and gave all the money and the grain to him. That was the system that was generally accepted by every culture in the world.

The only places that this has changed are in those nations that have been Americanized, where people have begun to grasp the truth that individuals have a right to the ownership of property. In America, it has always been a part of the ideal, the American dream. From the earliest years of settlement, people were encouraged in every way to seek to become landowners.

It used to be that only landowners were allowed to vote. It may seem like discrimination today, but it was considered a motivation by the government to get people to own property. Of course, in early America, it was easy to do. You could homestead property by piling rocks on four corners and signing the papers (or marking an "X" if you couldn't write). To own land, all you had to have was a willingness to work and develop the land. People who were lazy didn't own property. People who took the trouble to work their land were ambitious. Owning land indicated that you were a person of accountability, discipline and responsibility. That was the dream and in America, it was easy to achieve.

Capitalism, by definition, is based on private effort with limited government interference. The bigger government becomes, the more difficult it is for capitalism to flourish. The danger of bigger government is that the opportunities available in the land of opportunity diminish as dependence on government increases.

> **The bigger government becomes, the more difficult it is for capitalism to flourish.**

The Social Security system is a good example. There is currently talk of privatizing the system, taking it out of the hands of government and putting it into the control of private business. The original system was set up by industrialists whose primary concern was having a large supply of worker bees for their factories who had no interest in personal advancement or wealth. They wanted people who would work for their entire lives for a relatively inflexible wage and, at the time of retirement, have perhaps $1,400 a month from Social Security to live on. It isn't enough to buy a house or a car. In fact, it's barely enough to buy food and rent an apartment.

Compare that with what might have happened if a Baby Boomer had taken all of the money that he paid into Social

Security over the last forty years and just dropped it into the stock market. As volatile as the market is, that money would still be worth three to four million dollars at retirement. The difference between those two is that in the first system, the government has taken responsibility for your retirement and in the second, you have your own responsibility. It is time for responsibility to come back to the individual. The government has only misused the money and spent it all.

I'm not using this example to try to stir up some political movement. Rather, I want to change some perceptions that we have had. People don't like accountability or responsibility. They don't actually want to be forced to make decisions and then have to answer for them. They would prefer that someone else do it all for them.

I see it in churches all the time. I preach that every person is accountable for his own decisions and actions. If I began to teach that God is the one responsible for everything and that He's going to just send you money and take care of everything without any effort on your part, the church would grow twice as fast. People want to be told that God will make them rich, but they don't want to be told that they have to do something first.

That is the reason so many people adhere to religious practices. They want someone to tell them exactly how to live. "Do this," and "Don't do that." All I would need to do to get the church to grow faster is give them a whole bunch of rules that remove all freedom of choice and they will come in droves. They don't want to be accountable for their behavior. They especially don't want to be accountable for their finances.

That isn't biblical, however. According to Scripture, you are accountable. If you commit sin, it will cost you. There is a price to pay. You have the freedom of choice, but that means that you are responsible for the choices you make. Every other world religion and many sects of Christianity are a form of government that steals personal accountability and personal freedom. But that isn't the way God set it up to work.

You have choice in every area of your life. You can choose whether you do something or whether you don't. You can choose heaven or you can choose hell. You can choose sickness or you can choose health. You can choose poverty or you can choose prosperity.

In America, there is nothing stopping you from gaining wealth. If you are not living there, it is not because the government is keeping you down and it is not because God wants you poor. It is for one reason only—you have chosen to ignore the opportunities that surround you. The whole system in America, as our Founding Fathers envisioned it, is set up to make us accountable. You have no excuse. The danger in refusing to be responsible is that we turn the accountability over to bigger and bigger government and then we lose the opportunities. We must be careful.

America has experimented with socialism before and the results were disastrous. In fact, America began as a socialist state. It didn't last very long. The original charter for the Jamestown settlement, signed in 1606, required that all the colonists pool their harvest so that everyone could take out of a common store as there was need. The result was that people started working less. They saw others who reaped the benefit of someone else's labor and they asked, "Why should I work so hard when someone else who isn't working at all will benefit from it?" As a result, in spite of the fact that the colony was surrounded by tremendous amounts of game and food and huge natural resources, the colonists nearly all starved to death. Only a fraction remained alive after the first year—38 out of 105. Nearly 90% died the second year.

The problem was solved when the governor, Sir Thomas Dale, in direct violation of the charter, assigned plots of land to each family and told them that they would only eat what they produced. "If you don't work, you don't eat." The colony became prosperous virtually overnight. People got motivated.

The people who financed the original charter thought that the failure was because so many of the colonists were not religious. They backed the Plymouth expedition a few years later and wrote the same requirements into the charter. Everyone would share equally in all produce. Their reasoning was that a group who were moving to the New World to found a Christian community, based on the Bible, would overcome the selfishness and lack of accountability that plagued the Jamestown settlers.

The result, however, was exactly the same. The colony nearly starved until Governor William Bradford, in direct violation of the charter, assigned plots of land to each family and said, "If you don't work, you don't eat." Production increased dramatically overnight. Everyone got motivated.

Free Market Competition

The last part of the definition of capitalism states that the prices, price of products, and the production and distribution of goods are determined by competition in a free market. A free market is essential and competition is critical. Competition is something that causes human beings to be motivated. If you take competition out of the picture, you de-motivate the individual. People tend to not work if they don't have to. Very few are self-motivated enough to give their best if there is no reason to excel.

In our school systems today, they are trying to do away with competition. Many want to get rid of the grading system. They don't want any winners or losers in sports activities. If we get people to grow up without any sense of competition, they will make good factory workers, be non-competitive, boring, and most importantly, willing to work for a wage throughout life and have nothing to show for a lifetime of labor when they retire.

> **People tend to not work if they don't have to.**

Competition is your primary motivation for success. It is what makes businesses sharper and better so they grow. Competition is critical to your children. It is critical to you.

The outsourcing of jobs to other countries has produced some interesting insights into how capitalism works. Many people are upset about the process, but consider a couple of facts. First of all, the outsourcing has brought a sense of prosperity and westernization to another nation. We might consider that under the heading of "giving." It influences those nations for the good.

Secondly, outsourcing forces us as Americans to become innovative and creative and it makes us come up with new ideas and new businesses. It forces America upward again instead of staying stagnant in a noncompetitive market. Unfortunately, we mostly just complain because it also forces us to become accountable and responsible.

There is a very interesting example of competition within the churches of early America that demonstrates the difference between dependence on the government and dependence on God. In early America, most of the states had an official church that was supported by the state taxes. In Massachusetts and Connecticut, for example, it was the Congregationalist Church. In Virginia, it was the Anglican Church. All clergy were paid salaries from the state government. If you happened to belong to some other church, such as the Baptists, you still had to pay tithes into the state church, whether you liked it or not.

After the American Revolution, it was decided to disenfranchise those churches and stop paying government salaries to church leaders. Devout Christian leaders all over the country predicted that America would be judged by God for abandoning the church.

Of course, America didn't abandon the church at all. The states just stopped giving preference to any one denomination. The result was that preachers couldn't depend on the government for their income. They had to actually preach well or people would just go to another church. They had to provide spiritual leadership that caused people to believe it was worth staying in that church. The result was a revival, known in history as the Second Great Awakening, which reached a level never experienced in America before and not equaled since. The Gospel spread everywhere. Competition became good for every denomination and proved that dependence on the state was not really very healthy.

Of course, competition also implies tolerance. When one group of people attempts to enhance their freedom at the expense of another's freedom, you have a form of socialism that is detrimental to the freedoms that America cherishes. The ACLU has provided a good example. I believe in civil liberties and that was the reason for originally forming the ACLU. It started out with good intentions.

Where the error has crept in is in the desire to restrict the right of expression for everyone else. The freedoms that they try to protect for themselves are just as valid for everyone else. They are stealing my freedom when they force the removal of a nativity scene just because it offends them. When they do that, they offend me. That doesn't mean that we will remove them. It means that we will learn tolerance.

Everyone has a choice. You can choose to believe and you can choose to not believe. You can choose poverty. Nobody is going to make you get rich. You have the freedom to speak out against prosperity. You can write all the books that you want to try and discredit the prosperity message. If you really want to be poor, I'll be happy to take any money that you want to send me. I'll put it to good use doing God's work and you'll be as poor as you can be.

There is a movement in the church to keep people poor but it really just reflects a movement in America that is anti-capitalistic. It is an expansion to bigger government, financed by the wealthy to take care of the poor. It's ideal to punish the productive rich by increasing taxation in order to soften the lives of the lazy, unproductive poor, which bankrupts the capitalistic economy and quenches the motivational spirit of the productive. The freedoms that make America different will not survive long if that trend continues. We need to stop it now and start doing things God's way.

The Caste System

Most societies have a caste system of some sort. A caste system means that there are social classes. Typically, in most nations, there has always been a small class of aristocracy and a very large poor class with a small middle class of businessmen and merchants. The aristocrats have fed off of the labor and the work of those in poverty.

In most nations, it is pretty easy to define the classes. They don't mix with each other very much. You learn your class and you stay in it. The system is designed to keep the poor in their place—and poor.

It is easy to get caught up in all of that, even in America. There is an attempt to maintain a kind of class structure, though it is more subtle than in most nations in history. It is more of a psychological effort to keep the poor thinking that they always have to be poor, that there is no chance of ever changing it. That isn't the real America, however. What makes America different is that anyone can move to the highest class if he wants to work for it.

If you go back a couple of hundred years or more, typically, the lowest classes were not even allowed to look into the eyes of the upper classes. They were expected to maintain their position and not complain about it. In America, however, the lowest classes can look at the richest and say, "I can get there, too." America broke the caste system.

> **That is God's plan, that everyone become successful.**

I said earlier that capitalism is a biblical idea. It is also anti-caste. Jesus set out to break the caste system by bringing everyone up to a higher level. He showed up with a message that said, "I want everyone to prosper." He ministered to the rich and poor alike without distinction. He sought to bless everyone the same way. That is God's plan, that everyone become successful.

I experienced this transformation in my own life. I went from being ultra poor to where I am today. And I'm not finished yet. I broke through the system where I toil for the soil and I got to the place where the soil is toiling for me.

God is no respecter of persons. Anyone can do this. It doesn't matter what your education level is. It doesn't matter where you came from. Many have come from other countries because they saw the opportunities in America and often, those are the people who are taking the most advantage of the opportunities rather than people who were born here. It doesn't matter. It's available to anyone who is willing to take it, anyone motivated enough to break out of the caste of poverty and pursue the wealth God intends all of us to have. It's there for anyone who is willing to embrace God's plan and become prosperity minded. God wants you to start risking a little bit and start utilizing your faith to begin to believe what He says is available for you. Once you believe it, you're heading in the right direction.

CHAPTER 2:

Get Educated

During the past Christmas season, I had no greater joy than giving away virtually thousands of dollars to people I knew who were in need. I blessed them and made their Christmas that much better. It really didn't matter what I got in return. That had no bearing on the joy of giving. The real joy comes out of seeing them enjoy what I was able to give. The real joy comes out of being able to be a blessing.

I believe it is God's plan for us to have too much for the purpose of affecting the lives of others and thus building His Kingdom. When you have too much, it is easy to give whenever there is a need. It needs to be a concept and a conviction planted deeply in our hearts. It is not for greed or for selfishness, but it is so that we can share the life that God has given us.

As we saw in the last chapter, the freedom of choice is an integral part of capitalism. It is not that common elsewhere in the world. It is something that was birthed in America from the beginning. It is a part of biblical truth.

Any religion that steals your freedom of choice or your freedom of responsibility is a form of corrupt government. Never forget that. You have the right to choose right or wrong. Do not give up that freedom of choice by giving up your accountability and responsibility. Accountability is the only thing that will ever cause you to grow. If you can constantly blame God or someone else for everything, you will never grow. It is only when you accept responsibility and accountability for life that you will grow as a person. Only then will you be able to succeed at anything that you do.

... the Bible is about choice and with choice comes a responsibility to learn problem solving.

It is with this in mind that I want to discuss the education system in America today. We need to recognize what education is. From cover to cover, the Bible is about choice and with choice comes a responsibility to learn problem solving. Virtually all of the stories that we know from the Bible involve some degree of problem solving. God came to Noah and said, "It's going to rain. So you have a problem to solve. You're going to need a boat and you're going to need to get two of each animal to take on the boat." God helped, but Noah had to solve the problem.

Goliath taunted the Israelite army and everyone stood around scared. David stepped forward and solved the problem. Everything in the Word of God is about problem solving. The more we understand, the better equipped we are to solve problems. In fact, it is impossible to be an overcomer or more than a conqueror if you do not have the ability to solve problems. That's what overcoming means. You meet an obstacle and you figure out how to get past it.

When we talk about education, we need to make a distinction between being educated and being intellectual. There are plenty of people out there who have been through decades of school

> **The educated are problem solvers. The intellectuals are nothing more than problem finders.**

and are very smart but don't have an ounce of common sense. They couldn't solve a problem if their lives depended on it. They know a lot of information, but it doesn't translate into success in everyday life.

The educated are problem solvers. The intellectuals are nothing more than problem finders. Being educated has nothing to do with school. In the words of Mark Twain, "I have never let my schooling interfere with my education." Please understand that I believe in schooling. I'm not saying that we should stop going to school. There is much benefit from it. But schooling will not teach you what you need for life. Schooling will not teach you how to find the right mate. Schooling will not teach you how to be married. Schooling will not teach you how to raise emotionally healthy and successful children. It will not teach you how to maintain relationships. It will not teach you how to gain great wealth. It will teach you facts and information, but it will not teach you how to use that information.

An educated person has the ability to create new things,

new experiences and new ideas. An intellectual has the ability to criticize and to use created things. An intellectual will hug trees but will live in wooden houses. He will fight to keep you from digging for oil because of the effects on the environment, but he will drive an automobile. He will protest atomic energy, but he will still turn on his light switch.

Intellectuals live in the past. They use the present, but they cannot change the future. They learn a mass of facts, but are unable to solve problems.

We probably all asked the question when we were in school, "Why do I have to study this?" My boys frequently came home and complained about some of the subjects that they were sure they would never use at any time in life. Not many of us have ever used algebra or physics since graduation. Why should we waste our time studying it?

The truth is that the benefit is not in the information. It is not about what you learn. It is about learning to learn. If you develop the ability to learn what you don't want to know, you will be able to learn what you want to know. And you will be able to learn what you need to know to solve problems. You will learn how to think. That is what true education is.

For too many, they neglected to learn that important skill. They memorized just enough facts to pass a test and remembered them just long enough to get the grade. They never got into the habit of actually learning. They just memorized. Intellectualism is nothing more than going to school so that you can get a piece of paper that will make it easier for you to get a job. It will do that for you, but it will not teach you to solve the problems necessary to gain great wealth.

Booker T. Washington is a person in our history who is probably not remembered enough. He changed black history because he understood

Thomas Edison solved one problem and it changed the world.

the difference between schooling and education. He trained and changed generations because he understood the importance of education. Many of the things he said indicate clearly that he knew more was needed than just schooling if students were to truly succeed in life. Here are a couple of quotes from Booker T. Washington.

Success is to be measured not so much by the position that one has reached in life as by the obstacles which he has had to overcome while trying to succeed.

In other words, it doesn't matter where you get in life. It's about the problem you solved. How big was the thing you had to deal with?

The world cares very little about what a man or woman knows; it is what a man or woman is able to do that counts.

What you do is the thing that makes the difference. Can you solve a problem? If you looked into the world and solved one problem that would change people's lives, you would have too much money. Thomas Edison solved one problem and it changed the world. No one's lifestyle was the same after that. All you have to do to succeed in life is become a problem solver. Bill Gates solved one problem— Windows.

The great danger in America today is that we are turning out intellectuals but we're not turning out educated people. There is a massive increase in counseling, unprecedented numbers of psychologists and psychiatrists, and there's an influx of people going to get counseling, hoping someone will solve their problems for them, because they have never learned to solve problems themselves. They are lost in life without someone to help them. I'm not against counseling. When you need help, you need help. But the goal of counseling, to be successful, has to be teaching people how to solve the problem. Otherwise, they will stay in counseling for the rest of their lives and never change. If they learn to solve the problem, they won't need counseling anymore.

Our brains are capable of memorizing the entire *Encyclopedia Britannica* from A to Z, every single word in every single volume. You could learn fifteen languages and still only be using a fraction of your brain's capacity. It is said that Einstein only used about 20% of his brain. The average American uses about 8%. Think what the possibilities would be if we could tap into that unused capability, if we could just double our present ability.

The secret is to realize that it is not about going to school. That is not what makes you better educated. School will not make you wealthy. I finished twelve years of elementary and high school. Then I went to four years of college and into a master's program after that, then a doctorate program for thirteen years. I have twenty-nine years of college and, after all of that schooling, I still didn't know how to be married. I still didn't know how to raise children. I still couldn't make enough money to do much more than get by. I never learned from school how to solve problems. I had to have an education, not school. Benjamin Franklin, in his best sarcasm, described the difference between schooling and education:

> *He was so learned that he could name a horse in nine languages; so ignorant that he bought a cow to ride on.*

There is a simple logic problem by an unknown author that may help you determine just how educated you are. Most have difficulty with it. On a piece of paper, make three rows of three dots, as shown below. The object is to connect all nine dots with four straight lines without ever lifting the pencil from the paper.

The solution actually seems quite simple when you see it, but most people can't figure it out. The problem is that schooling has never taught us to think outside the box. We are limited by the imaginary border that the dots provide. We've been trained to stay within the boundaries. An educated person can think past those limitations and come up with the solution.

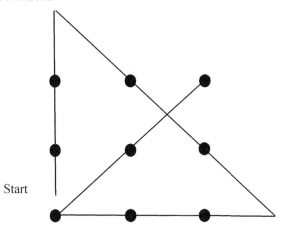

Start

Schooling has caused us to close off the creative side of our brains. That will make you an excellent worker, but you'll never get outside of the box. You will live your life making someone else rich and retire with nothing.

The Education of Jesus

Jesus was educated. He was also intellectual. Luke gives us an interesting picture of the years during which Jesus was learning. His parents had taken Him up to the Temple with them for Passover. When they left, they traveled with a group of relatives and acquaintances and didn't realize that Jesus wasn't with them until they were a day's travel away. They went back looking for Him and, three days later, located Him in the Temple grounds.

> *Now so it was that after three days they found Him in the temple, sitting in the midst of the teachers, both listening to them and asking them questions. And all who heard Him were astonished at His understanding and answers* (Luke 2:46-47).

The teachers that it refers to were the most learned rabbis and scribes of Israel. It was the custom for them to gather in the

Jesus was educated. He was also intellectual.

Court of the Gentiles during the week of Passover to debate and discuss a variety of subjects from the Scriptures. People usually gathered to hear these very learned and intellectual discourses. It was there that Jesus was listening and learning all that He could. He asked many questions and showed a level of understanding that amazed everyone who heard Him.

From this we can see that Jesus was intellectual, even at the age of twelve. He had studied the Scriptures. He knew the Old Testament backwards and forwards. Yet He seems to have not quite understood the meaning of "Honor your father and your mother." I'm not saying that Jesus sinned. We know that He didn't. But Luke describes a process of learning that is summed up in the last verse of Luke 2 with the words, "And Jesus increased in wisdom and stature." He was 100% God, but He was also 100% man and He had to learn things as He grew.

When Jesus' parents found Him, of course, His mother confronted Him and He willingly submitted to her authority and went with her. This was a

You can read through the Bible in a year and still have nothing.

moment of Jesus gaining understanding. For the next eighteen years, He became educated. He was intellectualized by the age of twelve, but He then had to learn how to learn. He knew the Scripture. Now He moved into understanding the Scripture and applying it.

That is what the body of Christ needs to learn to become problem solvers. Too many have intellectualized the Bible to the point that they can't understand it any more. You can read through the Bible in a year and still have nothing. You can memorize book after book, but until you get *rhema* revelation from that Word so that it becomes applicable to your everyday life, it is only an intellectual exercise. It won't help you solve any problems in your life because you will never figure out how to apply it to where you live. You are lacking education. Jesus was both intellectual and educated. He grew in wisdom.

And Jesus increased in wisdom and stature,
and in favor with God and men (Luke 2:52).

The word "wisdom" that is used here is *sophia*. It means thoughtful, discreet, practical, skilled, both worldly and spiritually. That means that Jesus understood the ways of the world. He had practical skills and He grew in them.

The word "stature" is *helikia*. It refers to specific time in life, meaning partly that He had grown in life, but more importantly, He had come to maturity. It meant that He had reached the position where others were more important than Himself.

Then it says that He grew in favor. "Favor" is the word *charis*. It is usually translated "grace." It meant that He possessed the qualities that are associated in the Bible with grace. He was thankful, happy, gracious and educated with the tools He needed for success. Jesus came out of His childhood educated and He changed the world with new ideas like, "Grace, not law," and, "Life, not death," or, "Health, not sickness," and, "Joy, not sorrow." These were new ideas for the world, new experiences that began to change generation after generation and are still changing the world today.

Jesus was educated and now you have the mind of Christ. One new idea, one problem solved, and you can change whole generations. Become educated. Jesus was.

Train Up a Child

Let's take this idea of education and begin to apply it to business. There is a principle that has worked throughout history; in fact it was at work before there was history.

In the beginning, God created heaven and earth. The Holy Spirit hovered over the face of the deep, waiting for the word to be spoken. Then God said, "Let there be light." The light was really enlightenment and the power of reason and at that point, Jesus showed up. We know that He was involved in creation from John 1:10. That is, in a very simple description, the beginning of the world.

The principle that I want you to see is this. God had the idea. Jesus put the program together. The Holy Spirit did the work. There was a distinct process to making it happen.

If I can use my own ministry as an example, the same principle holds true. As the senior pastor, I have an idea. I share it with my wife, Maureen, and my sons, Scot and Jason, who oversee the church administration. They put the program together and then they share it with the staff. The staff does the work.

The problem with many business owners is that they try to create the idea, formulate the program and do the work all by themselves. You'll never do it without the help of others who are strong where you are weak. This is true for anything you try to build. You cannot build a church, a business or a ministry without understanding this principle. No matter how good an idea is, if you cannot solve the problems of how to implement it, no one will ever benefit from it. A big part of the problem solving process involves working with other people so that the work actually gets done.

The ancient Greeks were probably the greatest intellects in history. We still study the philosophy that they wrote thousands of years ago. They studied everything. They would sit around in council for weeks at a time, discussing just how high "up" could be. Such information did not have practical application to life, however. That society does not exist anymore because it failed to solve problems necessary for survival. The memorization of facts will not make you successful. In the words of historian and writer Henry Brooks Adams, "Nothing in education is so astonishing as the amount of ignorance it accumulates in the form of inert facts."

Again, there is nothing wrong with schooling. Get a degree. It is useful. But also make sure you get an education. Make sure you learn to think. Learn to be a problem solver. This is not an indictment of the school system. It is an encouragement for you to go beyond what you learn there. Notice what Proverbs says about raising children.

> *Train up a child in the way he should go,*
> *And when he is old he will not depart from it*
> (Proverbs 22:6).

This verse is talking about education, not schooling. It does not say, "Send your child to school so that they can train him." Education is not actually the responsibility of the school system. It is the responsibility of the parents. We are to train our children in the way they should go. In other words, we are to teach them how to live their lives happily and effectively. That means that we have to train them in things like respect and to not be selfish, to have self-control and self-discipline. This training starts from the moment they are born. Toilet training is a form of self-control. Teaching them to feed themselves is a part of that training. Everything you do with a child should be training. You are where you are because of your training.

My dad was a very wise old lumberjack. He never finished eighth grade, but he had a great education. He trained me to think for myself and figure out what was right and what was wrong.

When I was in the eighth grade, for example, I had a teacher who just happened to live with us. I didn't like him much because he took my bedroom. On one occasion, we were in Physical Education class playing volleyball. This teacher slammed a ball down and hit a girl on my team, giving her a bloody nose. Some words came out of me that I will not repeat now, but in essence they said, "What are you trying to do? Kill somebody?"

Of course, those words were not very well received. He pulled me to the side and bawled me out thoroughly and, since he stayed with us, my dad naturally found out about it. My dad took me aside and sat me down. He said, "Son, you probably did a right thing the wrong way because he was probably in the wrong for what he did, but that's not your position, nor is it your place to correct the authority. Do you understand that?"

I replied, "Yeah, I understand that."

At that point, he could have said something like, "What do you think you should do?" The point is that kids don't really know what they should do. Had Dad asked that question, that would not have trained me. I would have told him that I needed to get an equalizer and beat the teacher. But my dad had education. He didn't say it that way. Instead, he asked, "What do you think is the right thing to do to correct the situation? What do you think is the right thing to do?"

We are to train our children in the way they should go.

There's a big difference between what I thought I should do and what was the right thing to do. I didn't like it at the time. It was the worst discipline I could get, because now I had to think about how to make it right. The only way I could do that was to apologize to the teacher. But that wouldn't be enough because I needed to apologize to him in front of the rest of the kids.

I waited until the next day and I put it off as long as I could, but finally, at the end of the class, I did it. I learned from that. I've never had a problem in my life submitting to authority and I have no problem apologizing when I need to. I also have no problem with problem solving. My dad was very wise in training me. That is what education is really all about.

Intellectualism will not train your kids for real life. Today, kids in school have to get a signed permission slip to get government milk, but those same kids can get an abortion without their parents knowing about it. That is the result of intellectualism without education.

Education should be a privilege. School is mandated, but that doesn't mean our kids are getting educated. It also doesn't mean that you were educated. You have to learn to think, learn to solve problems and learn to get outside of the box. It is the only way that you will succeed in life and do anything more than just get by. Education is a prerequisite for having too much. Get educated.

CHAPTER 3:

The Purpose of Creation

I'm going to assume that if you've read this far, you want to gain too much, and that by now you've examined your motives and, if they were not right, you've put them in order. The first thing that we have to do is to gain knowledge. Then we will figure out what to do with it. To begin this chapter, I want you to do an exercise that will help you get started. If you've never done this before, please take the time to do it now. It is designed to help you figure out where you are right now. Then you will be able to determine where to go next. Find out where you are financially.

First, we need to find where you should be. Take your age and multiply it by your gross annual income. For example, if you are fifty years old and you made $40,000 last year, you would get:

$$50 \text{ X } 40,000 = 2,000,000$$

Take that number and divide by ten. For example:

$$2,000,000 \div 10 = 200,000$$

That is the minimum that you should have in liquid net worth, meaning that if you sold everything you own, that is how much money you would have. In our example, this man should have $200,000 worth of possessions.

Now, total your net worth and see where you are at. Be realistic when you assess the value of your possessions. You may have spent $2,000 on a refrigerator, but it's not worth that much now. Be honest with yourself. If your total assets are worth less than the number you computed, then you've got some catching up to do. If you're above that number, then you're on your way.

If you're not up to the level that you should be, don't worry about it yet. That's why we're going through this, so that you can catch up. The time to worry is if you become content with less than you should. God wants you blessed to be a blessing. You can't do that if you're content with not enough. You can only do it if you have too much.

I don't know how anyone who has studied the Word of God could ever come to the conclusion that God wants people to be poor or that He would want you to remain in the caste system of poor and rich. I don't know how anyone could ever think that God wants people to be sick. If that were true, there would be no reason for prayer, no point to faith and no purpose in life. You'd be stuck where you are regardless of what you did.

To think in any of those ways means that you have not become educated in the Word of God. You may have read it, but you don't understand it and if you don't understand it, you'll never be able to apply it. There are so many examples in the Bible of God's blessing working in the lives of people who simply believed God enough to act on their faith.

In Genesis 12, we find the story of Abram. This was before his name was changed to Abraham. In Hebrew, the letters "AH" indicate great joy. God was about to add great joy to Abram's life, so He added a part of His own name and made him Abraham. He did the same to Sarai by changing her name to Sarah.

But that time hadn't quite come yet. First, God had to get the blessings into Abram's life. Then He could change his name. Abram had to get to the promises first. So He gave Abram this command.

Now the LORD had said to Abram:

"Get out of your country,
From your family
And from your father's house,
To a land that I will show you.
I will make you a great nation;
I will bless you
And make your name great;
And you shall be a blessing.
I will bless those who bless you,
And I will curse him who curses you;
And in you all the families of the earth shall be
blessed" (Genesis 12:1-3).

We see God's goal pretty clearly stated. The New Testament calls us the seed of Abraham, so these promises are ours, too. That means that His goal for us is to bless us so that we can bless others.

Abram had to make a choice. He could have stayed right where he was. He could choose to stay in his country, where he was, or he could move on to the promises that were somewhere else.

Everything about God's Word involves choice. You can choose to be blessed or you can choose to be cursed. You can choose to believe or you can choose not to believe. You can choose life or death. God will not force you to choose one way or another, but you do have to choose something. He does give us hints. "You can choose whatever you like, either life or death, but I'll give you a suggestion. Life is better."

As we look at some of the Hebrew words in this passage of Scripture, we can get a better understanding of them. "Get out" in the Hebrew means to "walk away from." There are some things that are strings and attachments from our past that we've been connected to that hold us back from what God wants us to have. We have to turn our backs on them and walk away. So God says, "Get out."

Now, if we took that literally, we would have to move to another country. That isn't the point of what God is trying to tell us. There is no other land of opportunity like America. The problem is that those of us born here don't seem to understand how to solve problems. It is foreigners who move here from third world countries who learn to solve problems. They've been solving problems their whole lives. They had to solve the problem of not having food and the problem of housing. They've struggled with so many problems that when they come to America, they see all kinds of opportunities and they rise to great wealth, while those who live here miss out through complacency and laziness. It is the complacency that we have to get out of.

Everything about God's Word involves choice.

The word "country" is interesting in this passage. It means, get out of your wilderness. We know that the Israelites were trapped in Egypt for 430 years. God set them free. He took them out of Egypt, a type of the world, and set them in the direction of the Promised Land. But they had to go through the wilderness. And they got stuck there for forty years.

In the wilderness, God miraculously provided for them. They sent manna every morning. There was a pillar of cloud by day to protect them from the sun and a pillar of fire by night to give them warmth. They had just enough food, just enough shade and just enough heat. There was just enough water to drink. If they tried to store food for the next day, it spoiled overnight. They had just what they needed and no more.

This is where we find most of the church today. God has set them free from the bondage of sin and pointed them in the direction of the promises, but they are in the wilderness. They have just enough to get by. They get the bills paid every month. There's enough food to eat. They have a little bit left over to go out to eat once in a while. But there is never any extra. They could not be a blessing to anyone else if they wanted to. There is just enough and no more.

God told Abram to get out of his wilderness, and He says the same thing to us today. Get out of your wilderness, your country. Get out of the place where there is never any extra. If you continue to live there, you will never have more than just enough. It's time to move on.

The second thing that God told Abram was to get away from his family. There is some destructive teaching around that encourages people to completely leave their families and never have anything to do with them again. That is not what this is saying. The Bible teaches you to leave the sin of your family, but you're supposed to be a light to them so that they can be won to the Lord. I've had relationships with people who are not born again that have lasted for thirty or forty years. I don't abandon them. I call them. I still project the light of the Gospel into their lives, giving them opportunity. But I haven't let their sin stay with me. I've left that behind.

> **Get out of the place where there is never any extra.**

The word "family," or "kindred" in the King James, refers to your pedigree or your heritage. Abram was to leave behind his pedigree. I've traced my ancestors back for many generations, as far as 1804. Gustaf Anderson had eighteen children and his wife died at the age of thirty-six. He never remarried.

What distinguishes all of the generations since is the poverty that they experienced. I can follow the lineage and the heritage of poverty through my father, my grandfather, his father, his grandfather and his father's grandfather. Poverty followed all of them. I had a pedigree of poverty. That was my heritage.

I had to walk away from my family. That does not mean that I broke all contact with them and never spoke to them again. It means that I left behind the pedigree of poverty and moved on to something better. Whatever the pedigree of your family, whether it be lust, greed, selfish ambition, pride or something else, you have to walk away from it or it will keep you from the promises of God. Leave that junk behind. Paul said it this way.

> *Brethren, I do not count myself to have apprehended, but one thing I do, forgetting those things which are behind and reaching forward to those things which are ahead, I press toward the goal for the prize of the upward call of God in Christ Jesus* (Philippians 3:13-14).

Next, we find the phrase "father's house." Abram was told to leave his father's house. Again, it is important to understand what this really means. Most cults attempt to get control of your life by telling you to leave your family. They want you to pull out of that security and come under their complete control. But that is not what God was telling Abram.

When I got married, I left my father's responsibility and I became responsible for my home and my family. But the Bible still says that I must honor my father and my mother (Exodus 20:12). That commandment says to honor them whether they are honorable or not so that my days might be long on the earth. I have a responsibility to see that they receive Jesus before they die. I have a responsibility to take care of them when they're old, whether they are saved or not, whether they are drunk or worse. It doesn't matter. I still have that responsibility. You don't leave your family. You honor them. You do leave family bondages. This is about leaving sin, not people. At marriage, I left my father's house, but I did not leave the relationship with him.

Then God told Abram that He would take him to a land that He would show him and that He would make Abram a great nation. The word "great" here means exceedingly, a whole lot of excess. The word "nation" means to rise up and increase. God says, "It is My will to give you excessive increase."

Then God said, "I will bless you." The word "bless" means favor, health, wealth, happiness, prosperity, joy-filled. God is saying that He wants to give you too much—too much health, too much joy, too much peace, too much money, too much wealth, too much prosperity.

Because of having too much, Abram would be a blessing. The same is true for you. God says that when you have too much, He will make you a blessing. But you have a choice whether to be blessed or not.

The word "blessing" here is a different Hebrew word

than "blessed." "Blessed" is highly favored, prosperous, wealthy, healthy and so on. But the word "blessing" means a liberal giver for God's purpose. In other words, God wants us to be blessed so that we can be liberal givers for His purpose, which is building His Kingdom.

This should bring us back to Psalm 122:9. We seek prosperity for the sake of the house of the Lord. God wants us to be blessed, but He wants us to seek the blessing for the right reason. If your motives are not right, you won't be able to handle a dollar, much less ten or a hundred or a million. We need to learn good stewardship now so that God can trust us with more.

Let's put all of this together. God told Abram, and through Abram, He told us, "In order to gain too much blessing, you have to walk away from the wilderness, the pedigree and the heritage of your family, the family bondage of poverty, sickness, confusion, of unrest, worry, greed, lust, and selfishness, and come to the good things in the promises of God."

The way of the world is to love money. The world seeks money because they believe money will give them things. God's plan, however, is for us to seek Him first and then He will give us things.

Unfortunately, the way of the world overflows into the church. We get born again, but we still have a lot of soulish junk hanging around and there is often still some love of money there. That is part of the wilderness that you need to walk away from to get to your Promised Land.

The way of the world is the love of money. The way

of the Kingdom of God is money for the love of people. When we love people, when we care about the lost and we care about training and teaching and bringing the Gospel worldwide, then we give.

Finding Purpose

Genesis 1 covers all of creation from start to finish. It gives an overview of all that God created and how He did it. Many people struggle with wondering why they were created, but Genesis 1 tells us. It is important to know, because without that purpose, there is no motivation for life. You have to have purpose in your life or you will dry up and die. You need purpose and direction and a goal so that you'll stay motivated.

God knew that, so He told us the purpose for which He created us.

> *So God created man in His own image;
> in the image of God He created him; male and
> female He created them. Then God blessed them,
> and God said to them, "Be fruitful and multiply;
> fill the earth and subdue it; have dominion over
> the fish of the sea, over the birds of the air, and
> over every living thing that moves on the earth"*
> (Genesis 1:27-28).

The first thing God did after creating the man and woman was to bless them. It should be clear by now that God wants people blessed. We keep finding it everywhere that we look.

From the beginning of creation, God blessed mankind.

Next, God told them to be fruitful and fill the earth. "Fill the earth" means to have children. That is so that we will have an inheritance to pass down to our children's children. So part of the purpose was procreation. This doesn't mean that you have to have children. It is your choice. But recognize that family is very important to God.

But there is more to man's purpose than just having children. The next thing God says is to have dominion over the world. To fully understand this, we need to look at the word "fruitful." It means much more than most people realize. It means to work for seed.

Everyone starts by working for seed. We start a job and we get a paycheck. In essence, we all start out working for money. God's ultimate plan is that we have an inheritance that goes to our children's children so that our money works for them and they don't have to work for seed. But we all start out working for seed.

That is not all that "fruitful" means, though. It also means to be productive or to build a business. In other words, we start with working for a seed, but God wants to take us to the place where a business begins to operate and we get so much money that money works for us.

We tend to think of business people as people who have money. How could they invest if they didn't have money? But it is a process that anyone can do. We work for seed. We begin with ideas and witty inventions, solving problems, and we develop that into business. I believe that the future of America is in private business. Because of the outsourcing of so many jobs as a result of technological advances, I believe that by the year 2015, 90% of Americans will own their own businesses. It is something that God told us from the creation of man that we should pursue.

The next word that we should look at is "multiply." Multiply means to take one and make more out of it. It is the process of increase. It is not just additional, but it is multiplied increase.

This is the whole concept of the Word of God as it is described in Malachi 3.

> *"Bring all the tithes into the storehouse,*
> *That there may be food in My house,*
> *And try Me now in this,"*
> *Says the Lord of hosts,*
> *"If I will not open for you the windows of heaven*
> *And pour out for you such blessing*
> *That there will not be room enough*
> *to receive it.*
> *And I will rebuke the devourer*
> *for your sakes,*
> *So that he will not destroy the*
> *fruit of your ground,*
> *Nor shall the vine fail to bear*
> *fruit for you in the field,"*
> *Says the Lord of hosts*
> (Malachi 3:10-11).

We give into the Kingdom of God and He multiplies

it. We bring our tithe into the storehouse, that there might be food there. The food feeds us that we might gain more information so that we can get more offering in. That becomes the seed that we plant in the Kingdom which then opens the windows of heaven. When your tithes and offerings open the windows of heaven, God pours out more blessing, which means that He pours out an opportunity for you to obtain great wealth.

We plant an offering in the Kingdom of God, but then it says that God will protect our crops from pestilence and protect our trees from casting their fruit. That means that we not only plant something in the Kingdom with tithes and offerings, but we have to plant something in the earth for Him to protect and to multiply.

> **We give into the Kingdom of God and He multiplies it.**

In Mark 4, the Parable of the Sower, we find that only 25% of those who plant seed actually multiply anything. One quarter planted seed but the devil stole it. Another 25% planted seed, but gave it up when trouble and persecution came. Another 25% got so far in debt with the deceitfulness of wealth that they couldn't invest and, as a result, became unfruitful. Three-fourths couldn't build a business.

This is where the message to get out of debt came from, but that message has a false teaching in it. Yes, you should get out of debt, but what is debt? Debt is when you owe more on something than you can sell it for. If you buy a house for $100,000 that is worth $120,000, you do not have a debt. You have a $20,000 asset that is making more and more money for you. You are using the world's money to make money.

On the other hand, if you buy a $1000 refrigerator on credit and take it home, by the time you get it out of the store, it's only worth about $200. That means that you have an $800 debt. Learn to recognize the difference between debt and investment.

> **The Word works when you believe it. It doesn't work just because you said it.**

The point is that God told us from the beginning of creation that He wants us to multiply. That means not only planting seed in the Kingdom of God, but also planting it in the earth so that there is something for God to multiply. Then it becomes an asset that pays a dividend. When the dividend surpasses the expense levels, then we no longer are working for money. Now it is working for us.

This principle is taught in many places, but one of the easiest places to find it is in Hebrews 3-4. It says that God had a people that He tried to take into the Promised Land, but they did not enter because of their unbelief. They could not enter His rest.

But He declares that the day is coming when that will change. That day is the Church Age. We enter in by our belief. By faith, we enter the promises of God. The problem is that so much of the Body of Christ has been trying to work the Word instead of getting the Word to work for them. The Word works when you believe it. It doesn't work just because you said it. You have to believe it. You can enter His rest by getting the Word to work for you.

The ultimate goal of everything from God's standpoint is to get the Word to work for us, to get money to work for us, to get to the point in every area of our lives that the soil toils for us instead of us toiling for the soil. This is the mystery of the ages that has been hidden for us, not from us. We need to grasp it and live it.

This is what breaks the curse. After sin, Adam had to work by the sweat of his brow, but God provided redemption so that the original plan could be restored. Part of our purpose at creation was to multiply. God didn't change that just because Adam sinned. In fact, He repeats it eight chapters later. Noah has the same command given to him.

> *So God blessed Noah and his sons, and said to them: "Be fruitful and multiply, and fill the earth"* (Genesis 9:1).

He says it again later in Genesis.

> *May God Almighty bless you,*
> *And make you fruitful and multiply you*
> (Genesis 28:3).

Jesus redeemed us from the curse and there is no excuse for not fulfilling our purpose to multiply. The promises are there for us anytime we want to believe them.

I think it is a worthy goal for the church to prosper to the point where people never have to go to the bank for a loan. They can get it from the church. God's people should be the primary lenders to the world. Then we would no longer be financing the world. We could finance the Kingdom of God instead.

It is time that we fulfilled our purpose. That means leaving behind our past heritage of poverty and going to a new country, the Promised Land.

"It's Not Fair"

We live in a land of equal opportunity. At least that is the ideal. We have been wrestling with equal opportunity in America since the time of the first settlers, especially during the last fifty years. We strive to provide equal opportunity for all races and for both men and women. We still haven't fully accomplished that, but that is our goal, and we constantly move closer to it. It is what our Founding Fathers sought when they wrote the Constitution. The opportunity is there for everyone. Some start a little farther from it than others, but anyone can reach it.

The equality that our Constitution speaks of is a biblical concept. The Bible clearly teaches equal opportunity for all. What we often fail to realize, however, is that the Bible doesn't promise equal ability. This is what Jesus taught in both Luke 19:11-27 with the Parable of the Ten Minas and in Matthew 25 with the Parable of the Talents.

In Luke, it says that a certain noble called ten servants

in and gave each one of them one mina and then he left for a period of time. A mina was a measurement of money worth about three months wages for an average worker. That seems fair. Each got the same amount. That is equal opportunity.

When the noble returned, he called for the servants. The first had invested the mina and turned it into ten. The second invested and turned his mina into five. The third didn't do anything with the mina.

> *Then another came, saying, "Master, here is your mina, which I have kept put away in a handkerchief"* (Luke 19:20).

He had exactly the same opportunity as the first two, but he did nothing with it. The noble chastised him saying that he could have at least put it in the bank and gotten some interest. He commended the first two servants by calling them "good and faithful," but he condemned the third. The problem wasn't the opportunity, it was the willingness to do something with the opportunity. Nowhere else in Scripture does Jesus call anyone a good and faithful servant except in these two passages in Luke and Matthew where the servants multiplied what they had by doing all that they could with the ability that they had. God is very favorable to multiplication. It is His plan.

The noble then did something that makes people today cringe. He took the one mina from the third servant and gave it to the one who had ten. That just doesn't seem fair to us. We would give it to the one who only had five.

We have to get past worrying about what is fair and what is not. "Fair" is not a biblical concept. Some have more ability than others. There is equal opportunity, but not equal ability. The second servant did not have the same ability as the first. He only produced half as much. Jesus gave the extra mina to the one with the greatest ability. We usually do it the opposite way. We would take from the one who had ten and give to the servant who had one. That is not God's way.

I understand that we are supposed to feed the hungry and clothe the poor. That is part of being generous with what we have. But that is not what this parable is talking about. It is emphasizing the point that if you want to stop being poor, you have to learn to take the ability that you have and use it to multiply. If you only produce half as much as your neighbor, that's still more than 80% of the other servants. And Jesus will say to you, "Well done, good and faithful servant." He is pleased with multiplication according to your ability.

The story in Matthew is similar. A man was traveling to a distant country, so he called together three of his servants. In this case, however, he didn't give them each the same amount. He distributed according to their ability. To the first he gave five talents, to the second, two talents and to the third, he only gave one talent.

Again, this doesn't seem fair to us. We have been trained to believe that we should all get the same amount. If I took three people and said to the first, "I'm going to give you $10,000 to see what you can do with it," the second and third would expect me to do the same with them.

But God provides equal opportunity, not equal ability. They may not have had the same amount of money handed to them, but each servant had an equal opportunity to take what they had and multiply it. Just like the master in the parable, Jesus is interested in what we will do with our opportunity. Will we multiply or we judge and condemn? If you will not begin taking advantage of the opportunities that come to you, then you will lose.

God provides equal opportunity, not equal ability.

Much like the servants in Luke, these servants came with the results of their investments. The first doubled his five talents to ten. The second turned his two talents into four. The third did nothing with his but hide it. Predictably, the master was not pleased with him. He commended the first two servants with the words, "Well done, good and faithful servant," but the third was chastised. His talent was taken away and given to the servant who had ten. And then the master declared something that just doesn't sound fair, but it is biblical truth.

For to everyone who has, more will be given, and he will have abundance; but from him who does not have, even what he has will be taken away (Matthew 25:29).

The question is, for everyone who has what? More will

be given to the one who has a willingness to multiply what he has. This is not about being fair. It is about fulfilling your purpose to multiply what you have.

True education, the ability to solve problems, actually creates inequality—the inequality of individuality, the inequality of success, the inequality of talent, the inequality of genius. The question is not how much you are given to start with but what are you doing with what you have?

CHAPTER 4:

In the Midst of Wolves

Jesus frequently used the image of sheep to describe His followers. He said, for example, that He was the good shepherd and that His sheep know Him (John 10:14). There is great comfort in recognizing that Jesus is watching over us with the care that a shepherd bestowed on his sheep. We love to read Psalm 23 when we are in distress because it comforts us. "The Lord is my shepherd. I shall not want."

But there is a more sobering use of the sheep image that probably scares most of us. It is in Matthew.

> *Behold, I send you out as sheep in the midst of wolves. Therefore be wise as serpents and harmless as doves* (Matthew 10:16).

This just doesn't sound like something a good shepherd should do. We think of ourselves as helpless little white puff balls in the midst of snarling carnivores, who are ready to tear us to pieces. Why would Jesus send us into such a fatal environment? There must be something wrong with that picture.

That is how I felt about that verse for many years. It bothered me. But that was because I read it with knowledge, but not with understanding. I want to examine this a little closer. It can teach us some things that will help us get a better approach to business.

The first aspect of this verse is the environment where we are being sent. Most people work in a wolves' environment, for the most part. And for many, the just simplywant out.

Let me begin by saying that you create your own environment. God said, "Let there be," and He created the environment of earth. The second Adam, Jesus, has redeemed us to that position where we are able to create our own environment, no matter where we are.

...you have the power to create your environment.

You might think that you are a product of your environment. Your parents may not have created a good environment for you as a child, but now that you're an adult, you have the power to create your environment. You are the one who decides what gets into you and what doesn't get in. You don't have to allow anything in that you don't want. Your coworkers may use language that you don't like. They may tell jokes that are offensive to you. But you don't have to let the dirt in. Instead, you are to let the light out. Don't judge them, but love them. It isn't what you say to them, it is how you live your life that will make a difference.

I worked in the world for many years before I was in full–time ministry. I've been a college professor, a teacher from grade school through high school. I've worked in electrical, plumbing, sheet metal and welding. I've done air conditioning and quite a few other things. I've spent plenty of time working in the world.

No matter where I worked, it wasn't very long before they started calling me "Rev," short for "Reverend." I didn't tell them that I was a Christian. I didn't do anything or say anything. I just worked. I did my best. I started early, quit late and only charged for eight hours. I did everything the best that I possibly could. When I hit my finger with a hammer, I said, "Bless God," instead of other words that they were used to. It wasn't very long before they called me "Reverend."

It also wasn't very long before they started to ask me for help with their marriages or help with their kids. I still hadn't told them anything, but people know when they see light and they are drawn to it. Then you have an open door. You have the opportunity because you've loved them to a position. You don't do it by beating them over the head with a Bible. You can't do it with religious rhetoric. You don't accomplish that by judging them and telling them not to swear around you. You do it by living a godly life. Your life will create the environment.

With that in mind, let's look carefully at this verse so that we can understand what Jesus meant when He said that He sent us out as sheep among wolves. The word "send" means sent with purpose.

What is our purpose? From Genesis 1, we learned that our purpose is to be fruitful, multiply and fill the earth. In other words, build a business, plant finances into the Kingdom of God and into the earth and multiply your money so that you can leave a large inheritance to your children and in the process, prosper for the sake of the house of the Lord. That was the purpose in the Garden of Eden and it never changed.

> **If the wealth of the wicked is laid up for the just, they just have to go out there and get it.**

We are sent into the world with purpose. In order to get the wealth that God wants us to have, we have to learn to use the world system for our benefit. If the wealth of the wicked is laid up for the just, they simply just have to go out there and get it.

How do we do that? You go to a bank and you borrow as much money as they will lend you. Then you go and buy a piece of property, build a house, buy a house, buy something that you know you can sell for more than you paid for it. You borrow the money for 4% and then you make a profit of perhaps 20%. You give the bank back the 4% and keep 16% for yourself and for the Kingdom of God. We use the world system. We take advantage of it. We use the wisdom God gives us to multiply and increase.

We are sent out with purpose. But we are still sheep, right? Most people think of sheep as cute, helpless little balls of wool with eyes and legs. The Greek word here for sheep, *probaton*, means something very different, however. It means to walk forward, to advance, to go in front of, to be first.

In other words, God sent us out with the purpose of being first. That is what the rest of Scripture says, so it shouldn't surprise us. God said that He wants us to be above and not beneath, the head and not the tail. We can do all things through Christ who strengthens us. He wants His sheep to be first.

That's the leader of the corporation, not the mailroom guy. That's the owner of the business. That's the supervisor, the foreman, the one who can solve problems. God wants us to be first. I guess being a sheep isn't such a dangerous thing, after all. He sent us out as sheep among wolves because He wants us to be absolutely first.

The next word is "midst." We are in the midst of the wolves, in the midst of the world. The Greek word here means in association with, not equally yoked with, but first. We are to rise to the top. We are supposed to be first in the midst of the wolves.

Wise as Serpents

After telling us that He is sending us out as sheep in the midst of wolves, Jesus continues with a word of instruction about how to do it. The next word is "therefore." That means that He's about to give the answer. This is how you do it. You become as wise as a serpent and as harmless as a dove.

Most people, when they see the word "serpent," immediately think of the devil and assume that we're supposed to be as clever as the devil and do things his way. That's not what the passage means. We need to examine the words a little deeper.

"Wise" means sagacious, acute discernment, mentally put together, cautious in character, honest, having integrity, punctuality and the divine nature of God. When we go into the world, we are not supposed to do things the world's way. We should understand their way, but we act with honesty and integrity. It means to be educated, not just intellectual. It means to have the ability to solve problems.

You do have to understand the world. Wisdom implies that you do. You won't change the world unless you understand the world. You'll never make a dollar in the stock market until you understand that it's run by greed and lust. That doesn't mean that you have to become greedy and lustful. It just means that you understand how it works. You can use the world's stupidity to bring wealth into the Kingdom of God. You have to be wise as a serpent.

How wise is a serpent? The word "serpent" is very interesting. We usually think of the devil but the word actually means sharpness of vision, introspection. All Jesus was saying is that we should have introspection, which is a matter of understanding ourselves and dealing with issues we have inside. It means the ability to examine what is in us. Sharpness of vision means having a focused vision. Once you get a vision, you never let go of it. If the vision is to build a business, then you never hesitate. You pursue the vision that you have. You don't switch visions on a whim.

You stay focused.

Another thing about a serpent is that it is quiet. Christians tend to blab all of their ideas around until somebody steals them. A serpent is sly. That doesn't mean being dishonest, but it does mean using some discretion.

A serpent is also patient. He can sit there coiled up all day, waiting for a rabbit or a gopher to come by. He is patient, but he's also ready to strike instantly when the opportunity comes. Everyone has opportunities, but most of the time, we're not ready for them. To be ready means that you are ready to move. Your credit is good. You've got the loan in hand. You can go down to the bank and in one day, make it happen. If your credit is lousy and it's gong to take six months to clean it up, you'll miss the opportunity. You need to clean it up now so that you are ready.

We should also note that snakes are ok with too much. They always eat too much. Have you ever seen a skinny little snake swallow a gopher? He ends up with a great big lump in his stomach. Snakes are okay with too much.

So being wise as a serpent does not mean being deceitful. It means having discernment and character so that we can understand how the world works. It means being introspective so that we can deal with our own issues. It means getting clear vision and focusing on it. It means having discretion about where and when we share our ideas. It means being patient.

Harmless as Doves

We are also supposed to be harmless as doves. When we picture a dove, we usually just think of a little bird that sits on the fence and makes a mess. The word "harmless," however, has a couple of meanings. Like "sheep," it means to be first. Considering how many times we run into that concept, we should really believe that God wants us to be first.

In addition, "harmless" means to advocate, negotiate, to compromise. That doesn't mean that we compromise the Word. That is something that we should never do. But it does mean that we solve problems peaceably when possible. When there's a problem, we're able to solve it with the power of our tongues. We use words. We negotiate. If someone takes you to court, the Bible says to do everything you can to settle the issue before you get there. If it's possible to solve the matter peacefully, then do it. There may be times when you can't do that, but we are supposed to do everything that we can.

With the understanding of these various words, we get a very different picture of what Jesus was trying to convey to us. This would be the Anderson paraphrase of Matthew 10:16.

> *I am sending you with purpose. Be fruitful and multiply. Watch your back in association with the world. Go forward. Don't back up. Be first. Use practical, spiritual and worldly skills. Discern. Keep focused and maintain a strong vision. Be patient but ready to strike first. Use*

the power of your tongue to resolve problems.

This same instruction is included in Luke, but with very slight differences.

> *Go your way; behold, I send you out as lambs among wolves* (Luke 10:3).

Here, Jesus uses the word "lambs" instead of "sheep." That would seem to indicate even greater helplessness, a baby sheep instead of an adult. But the word "lamb" has a whole different meaning.

Again, it says that we are sent, meaning that He sends us with a purpose, to be fruitful, multiply and be first. But the word "lamb" means an anchor, the heavy weight, the exasperator of sin.

We are not only responsible to reach people for Jesus; we are also responsible to take back this earth.

Exasperator means to thoroughly annoy sin. So Jesus said, "I send you out into the world to be first, to exasperate sin and to show them that My way is the right way, that My way has the power and that your way does not." Jesus sends us to take back the land that had been taken from Adam. We are not only responsible to reach people for Jesus; we are also responsible to take back this earth. When He calls us lambs, He means that we are to be the anchor, the heavy weight, the exasperator of sin, to thoroughly annoy sin, to bring an end to the wolves' control of this earth and take dominion and authority in the spirit and in the natural.

We need to grasp this understanding that God wants us to redeem the whole world. It is not just a matter of getting people to heaven. That is very important, but it is only the beginning. Paul said it to the Corinthians:

> *Therefore, if anyone is in Christ, he is a new creation; old things have passed away; behold, all things have become new. Now all things are of God, who has reconciled us to Himself through Jesus Christ, and has given us the ministry of reconciliation* (2 Corinthians 5:17-18).

When it says that all things are of God, it means all things that have been created. What did He create? It was more than just people. It included the earth, the moon, the stars—everything. Through Jesus, God has reconciled all things to His Kingdom.

But then it says that we have been given a ministry of reconciliation. We are also to reconcile all things. That doesn't just mean people. We are to win people through the blood of Christ, who has reconciled us to God, but then, there are all the other things that we are to reconcile as well. We are to take back the earth, take back what was lost. That means taking back the education system, the political system and the financial system. We are to reconcile people and the earth and to have dominion.

Wolves in Sheep's Clothing

Since we are talking about wolves, I need to add another word of caution. Not all wolves are out in the world. There are some who find their way into the church. Jesus warned about them.

> *Beware of false prophets, who come to you in sheep's clothing, but inwardly they are ravenous wolves* (Matthew 7:15).

There are basically three types of people in church. There are sheep, goats and wolves. The sheep are those who are committed to the church and to each other. The goats are relatively harmless, but they also don't do much. They tend to like eating on the other side of the fence so they come and go. We milk them while they are there but they don't usually stay long.

The wolves are another matter. They are there to devour sheep. They like high positions. They like to be up where they can be noticed. They like to pick out the weak sheep and devour them. So Jesus said to beware of them. He calls them false prophets. These are religious pretenders. They are filled with deceitful words that they use in an attempt to get people to follow after them, rather than pointing them towards Jesus. We are to watch out for them.

How can you spot them? There was a day when Jesus was walking along and he saw a fig tree that had leaves (Matthew 21:18-22). Leaves mean that the fruit should be ready. The purpose for the leaves is to protect the fruit from the sun.

Jesus went to the tree to get something to eat but when

He looked, there was no fruit. It was a false prophet. It prophesied that it had fruit, but it didn't.

This is the way to identify the wolves in your midst who are false prophets. Examine their fruit. Do they have healthy, long-lasting relationships? Do they minister life to people? Do they constantly attack your friends in order to draw you to them? They pretend to be Christian guides but their purpose is selfishness. They want to control you as a sheep. They want to abuse you as a sheep.

We need to treat these wolves with the same wisdom and discernment that we treat wolves in the world. Beware of them. Do not let them keep you from being first and focusing on your vision.

CHAPTER 5:

What If?

There is a process that we go through as we progress in life. I've alluded to it already, but I want to look closer at it before we move on. It is summed up in Proverbs.

> *The Lord by wisdom founded the earth;*
> *By understanding He established the heavens;*
> *By His knowledge the depths were broken up,*
> *And clouds drop down the dew.*
> (Proverbs 3:19-20)

The last part of this passage describes the breaking up of the depths. That is when the water came forth from the earth and from the heavens and destroyed the earth. It came when God found sin on the earth and saw that every attitude and every thought was only evil. The only survivors were Noah and his family.

We see what God did with knowledge. He destroyed the past and produced the future. That's what God wants to do in each one of us. In order to come into too much, we've got to destroy some things that are in our past. We've got to get rid of a poverty mentality, get it out of our hearts, our perceptions and our attitudes. You may have been a victim of circumstances in the past, but it's time to get over it. It's time to let that be destroyed by the Word so that you can get on to the good things that God has ahead. That is done by knowledge.

By understanding, God established the heavens through the process of salvation in Christ Jesus. You begin with knowledge. That is the change process. You then move to understanding, which is when you understand what you gained through knowledge. Many stop with knowledge and never gain understanding. They never figure out how the things work. They just have information.

From understanding, we have to move to wisdom. Just understanding what you know doesn't produce anything. When you begin to do what it is that you understand, you'll see great wealth come to your life.

This is the process that you need to follow. You need to become financially literate. You need to learn the information. Then you need to understand how the systems work, whether it's the spiritual system or the worldly system. But then, faith without works is dead, so you also have to do something. You have to take that understanding and apply it to real life. Take action.

A great example of this process is the life of Joseph. I want to take a detailed look at him and see how he rose from nothing to be the virtual ruler of the greatest nation in the world. There are numerous principles that we can glean from his life.

Don't "If" Yourself Out

Joseph didn't have prosperity just handed to him. He should have. His father was wealthy and he was in line to inherit a substantial portion of that wealth, but he ran into some problems along the way.

His brothers hated him. They sold him into slavery. He ended up as a servant to Potiphar. Then, just when things seemed to be going better, Potiphar's wife tried to seduce him and, when he chose the moral path, she made false accusations that resulted in his imprisonment. Joseph definitely had some obstacles to overcome. He could easily have resigned himself to his fate and said, "If only things had been different."

Don't "if" yourself out of the race. That is the greatest success stopper. It destroys incentive. It wrecks confidence. It ruins our adventurous spirit and it robs us of our dreams. On the plains of hesitation lie the bleached bones of thousands who, on the very threshold of victory, sat down to rest and while resting, died. "If" is a word of delay. It is a word of despair.

"If my boss didn't make me work so hard..."

"If I had more energy..."

"If I had more talent..."

"If I had more education..."

"If I had more money..."

"If I had more time..."

"If I had better health..."

"If I didn't have to work such long hours..."

"If" can stop you in your tracks and destroy your dream before you ever get close to it. Joseph had every reason to fail. But he had a dream that he never let go of. In his case it was actually a dream in which he saw his family, including his father and mother, bowing down to him. This was a picture in the natural of what would come to pass in the New Testament. Joseph was a picture of Jesus. His brothers represented the twelve tribes of Israel and the dream foreshadowed the time when every knee will bow at the feet of Jesus.

The day would come when Joseph's family would bow before him. Until that time, Joseph had a dream of a day when he would rise above his circumstances and have dominion.

One person committed to a dream is all that God needs to change the world. That's all it took when Abraham committed himself to the dream that God gave him. God told Abraham, "I'm going to give you a child and out of that child's seed, every nation will be blessed. Romans chapter 4 tells us that Abraham did not waver, did not leave faith, did not doubt. He hung on to the Word of God and as a result, it was counted as righteousness to him because he fulfilled the dream. And God changed the world through Abraham.

Moses had a dream that was birthed from the burning bush, a dream of delivering his people from Egypt. He led three million people out of bondage without a sword. He led them out with great wealth and great health. He fulfilled the dream that God put in him. He had plenty of obstacles, but he refused to let anything stop him. And God changed the world through him.

Noah received a dream from God to save creation. He was committed to it. What would have happened if Noah had started the ark but decided it was too much work and he wanted to relax instead? What if he had complained because he had to work more than forty hours a week and he just quit? He didn't

> **One person committed to a dream is all that God needs to change the world.**

do that. He kept at it and fulfilled the dream that God gave him. And it preserved humanity from destruction.

The world is changed through individual people who follow a dream. Martin Luther King had a dream. He dreamed of a world in which every race and color could come together, worship God in unity and love one another. That dream is being fulfilled because he was committed to it and never backed down. The world has changed because of it.

Jesus had a dream that He was going to redeem all of mankind. Peter came against Him and tried to talk Him out of it. Jesus just said, "Get behind me, Satan." He wouldn't be deterred from fulfilling the dream by anyone, not even a close friend.

Paul had a dream. On the road to Damascus, God spoke a dream into him to reach all of the Gentiles with the Gospel. He never backed away from that dream and as a result, God used him to change the world.

Dreams are critical to success. If you give up on your dream, you will never reach success. Joseph's uncle, Esau, was an example of someone who traded away what God had for him. He sold his inheritance to Joseph's father, Jacob, for a pot of stew. He didn't have a vision for where he could go. He became a type of those who have rejected their inheritance.

How many Christians are selling out their inheritance because they believe they should be poor? How many are selling it out because they think Jesus was poor? How many are selling out their future success because they are convinced that God has predetermined that they are to be sick and die young?

We are joint heirs with Jesus in all the promises of God. How could we believe anything different? Joseph had a dream that was founded in the promises of God. If your dream is not birthed from God's will, then you are in danger of following in Esau's footsteps. You need a God-given dream.

Let me give you an example. We now have a television generation that reflects more input from TV ads than from their parents. They have looked at solutions to problems in a way that is not healthy. They see problems solved by product rather than by behavioral change. They attempt to find cures for disease rather than doing something about what causes disease. They're looking for the effect, not the cause. They solve the problem of having unwanted children through abortion. I have another solution. It's called abstinence, self-control. They are looking for power without the principle.

This has produced a generation of people whose actions have lost control of their future. They have traded away their inheritance for self-gratification. They have no new ideas. They don't know how to solve tomorrow. They can't even solve today. They are seeking to make the world fair by putting everyone on the same level, giving every student the same "satisfactory" as a grade. They are creating a kind of caste system that no one can break out of. They want the government to take care of everything

How many Christians are selling out their inheritance because they believe they should be poor?

through social medicine and social security. They want to take from the successful and give it to those who will not work. They want all of the promises, whether they deserve them or not. This attitude permeates modern society and it destroys dreams.

The good news is that 95% of the people you meet in life will never do anything. You have no competition for success. They are looking for fair, but life is not fair. You know the truth so you can rise to the top. Just don't trade in your dream for a short-term fix.

The Bolshevik Revolution of 1917 dramatically changed Russia. The poor class rose up and killed all of the successful in an attempt to make everything level, to give everyone the same. They called it Socialism or Communism. Everybody was expected to share equally in all property. The problem was that when they killed the successful, they stole all motivation out of the hearts of everyone left, so no one pursued a dream. Why bother, when success will just be taken away from you and given to someone else who didn't work as hard? The system fell apart in eighty years. It could not sustain itself.

> **Joseph began with a dream and he never let go of it, regardless of his circumstances.**

Joseph began with a dream and he never let go of it, regardless of his circumstances. Has God given you a dream? Has He spoken something into your heart? Has He given you a talent, a race to run, a destiny to reach? Then commit yourself to it.

When I was seven years old, I made a decision. I remember it clearly, sitting in my bedroom. I said, "I want to make a difference because I lived." I don't think I was even saved at the time. My grandmother talked about Jesus and probably led me to the Lord, but I didn't have anything in my life to substantiate it. But I know that I had a dream in my heart and I know it came from God. I wanted to make a difference.

That ought to be the dream of every person's heart. You want your life to count for something. Get ahold of a dream and don't let go.

There is a story of a man who lived in Europe in the beginning of the nineteenth century. He dreamed of getting to America and he worked and saved to be able to afford his dream. For a couple of years, he saved every penny he could and finally, he was able to buy a ticket and board the ship.

It was almost a two-week trip in those days from Europe to America. He didn't speak the language so once on board the ship, he didn't really know quite where to go. He looked around and ended up down in the boiler room, which seemed to him to be nice and warm. He had packed enough food to last for the entire trip, along with some water.

Near the end of the trip, one of the ship's hands discovered him there and thought he was a stowaway. The man said, "No, I have a ticket."

The hand said, "But, sir, you have a stateroom that is yours. All your meals are paid for, the very best banquets and feasts. Why are you here?"

The man shrugged his shoulders and said, "I didn't know."

How many Christians are doing the same thing in their lives because they just don't know what God has prepared for them? They are walking the path of poverty because they don't realize God has promised them abundance. It's available, but they aren't living in it. They have traded their inheritance out of ignorance.

CHAPTER 6:

Your Greatest Enemy

Joseph was a type of Jesus. We will see many parallels between his life and the life of Christ. Joseph represented the life of grace. His father Jacob, later renamed Israel, represented the law. If you have the law operating in your life, you will never experience the promises that come through grace. Grace causes you to overcome every obstacle, as long as you believe the promises.

Joseph was thrown into a pit. Then he was raised from the pit and sold into slavery. He was thrown into a dungeon, but then he was raised from there. No matter where Joseph ended up, he rose from it. He always ended up on top. No matter what situation he found himself in, he always did the best. He was the best slave, the best manager, the best prisoner. He became the cream in every circumstance and rose to the top. He had plenty of obstacles, but he showed that any obstacle can be overcome.

The Parable of the Sower demonstrates the kinds of things that will try to keep you from reaching the promises of God. It is found in Mark 4. I'm going to paraphrase it a little to give you a better understanding of the meaning of the text.

In verse 14, it says that the sower sows the word. We receive a dream from God, a word from God. We receive healing from God, some promise that is for us. We sense that we have it. We think that we have it. The first thing that happened in the parable was that birds came and ate some of what fell by the wayside.

As soon as we think we've got it, the enemy comes immediately to steal it. Jesus got a word from God when He came up out of the water at His baptism. The Father said, "This is My Son in Whom I am well pleased." The first thing that happened was that the devil tried to steal that word from Him. Three times he tried to steal it. Each time, the devil started with the words, "If you're the Son of God..." He tried to take away the Word of God.

The enemy will come to you every time you get a dream. You start pursuing it and he will come to steal the dream from you. He will whisper in your ear and try to get you to doubt that it really was a dream from God. He tells you that you can't do it. He tells you that you're not educated enough, you don't look good enough, you're too old, you're too young, you're too this or too that. As soon as you believe him, you can't do it. You start telling your friends about your dream and they tell you the same thing that the devil said. Now you really don't believe it.

How did Jesus answer the devil? He went straight to the Word. He wouldn't say anything else. When the devil tells you that you can't do it, you answer with the Word. "I can do all things through Christ Jesus who strengthens me. I'm made in His likeness and image. I'm above and not beneath. I'm the head and not the tail. Sorry, Devil, but you lost."

The second place that seed fell was on stony ground. These are the ones who hear the Word and immediately receive it with gladness. They are excited about the dream. They are thrilled, but they have no root and they only endure for a short time. When tribulation and persecution arise for the Word's sake, they immediately stumble or they are offended.

They say, "I think I can," but as soon as they run into any obstacles, they lose sight of the dream. All they can see are huge mountains in the way. The dream appears too big, too hard, and they say, "I tried faith and it didn't work. I tithed but I still don't have any money. I guess it didn't work." They shoot themselves in the foot. The dream is stolen from them because they have no root, no depth.

When the devil tells you that you can't do it, you answer with the Word.

How should we answer when we run into obstacles? We go right back to the Word. It says that we can speak to the mountain, tell it to be cast into the sea and, if we believe, we will have what we say. No mountain should stand in the way of fulfilling our dreams.

The third place where seed fell was among thorns. These are the ones who hear the word, but the cares of the world and the deceitfulness of riches and the desire for other things enter in and choke the word and it becomes unfruitful.

These are people who are not able to produce anything. They have received the word and they say, "I think I can," but they get distracted. They see something that somebody else has and their credit card says that they can have it, too. They get it, but they don't actually own it. The deceitfulness of keeping up with other people who can afford it causes them to become unfruitful. They'll never have too much because they spent all of their money trying to have what they couldn't afford before they could afford it.

If you would wait on God and apply the process of an investor until your investments surpass your expenses and your dividends are coming in, you can begin to buy without debt. That is the deceitfulness of wealth. Learn to do it God's way and learn patience.

The last place that seed fell was on good ground. This is those who hear the word, accept it and bear fruit, some thirty to one, some sixty to one, and some a hundred to one. This is God's group. He said, "If you are patient and persevering, you will rise to the surface and become number one."

The Danger of Comfort

All of these things can conspire to rob you of your dream. Like Joseph, you need to hang onto the dream, no matter what happens. Joseph was attacked by his brothers, but there was an even greater problem that stood in the way of his dream. Before all of that happened, he was comfortable. He had a dream of what God wanted to do, but he was happy just sitting around at home. He wasn't actually doing much of anything. That was part of the reason his brothers hated him. They were doing all the work.

Comfort will rob you of your dream. To get you out of your comfort, God often allows your circumstances to make you uncomfortable.

The Bible often uses the analogy of an eagle. Mom and Dad eagle build a nest on a very high point of a cliff or a tall tree. They intertwine sticks that they break off and they weave them together into a huge nest. Then they pull feathers out and they coat the inside of the nest so that it will be soft and plush and comfortable. Then they lay their eggs and wait for the eaglets to hatch.

Comfort will rob you of your dream.

The baby eagles live in that nice warm nest, all snuggly and nice. It is soft and the wind can't get in. They just hang out all day while Mom and Dad bring them food and take care of them. They can see their parents soaring around through the clouds and they think that it would be great to do that someday, but for now, it's really comfortable in the nest. They get a dream, but they don't do anything to pursue it because it is so comfortable where they are, kind of like people who stay out in the wilderness.

Then the day comes when Mom and Dad decide it's time for the eaglets to fly and start taking care of themselves. They look at their kids and say, "You're fat enough." They start pulling out the feathers from the nest lining and throwing them away. It isn't long before the cold wind starts to blow inside the nest. The babies start to shiver a little bit.

Then the twigs start poking them. The nest starts to get uncomfortable. It isn't long before they can't stand it much more. They hop up on the edge of the nest. Mom looks at them and suddenly slaps them in the back and knocks them off the nest.

Now they have to do something. It's instinctive. They start flapping their wings out of desperation. They're headed for the ground.

Their mom doesn't abandon them. She waits a little bit and then dives down and grabs them just before they hit the bottom. She brings them back to the nest and sets them on the edge. She gives them a little time to settle down and then she smacks them again and they do it all over again. She keeps doing that until they learn to flap their wings enough to come to a landing on their own. Before long, they are soaring like eagles.

God puts a dream in our hearts and, sometimes, the only thing that gets us out of the comfort of the wilderness is a situation in our lives that makes us move, an external force that drags us out of our comfort zone. God doesn't hurt us, but He does use the attacks of the enemy to motivate us.

We need to keep moving forward. We don't want to be a stagnant pool. We want to be running water that has life in it. A stagnant pool stinks. We have to be cautious and wary of comfort and the dangers of what it can do to us. Sometimes it takes an external force to get us moving.

I can tell you that you ought to eat right and exercise. You would probably agree with me, but that doesn't mean that you will take the trouble to do it. But when the doctor says, "If you don't change how you eat, you're going to die," you suddenly get motivated. I've known people who wouldn't change even then. They had to go through a heart attack before they would change. You need to change before the external force moves you. It's a lot easier.

Many people know that they are in financial trouble and they still don't do anything about it. It is amazing how often people come to me and say, "They're going to repossess my house tomorrow."

My question is, "You knew that last month. What did you do to get ready for it? Did you get another job to bring in more money? Did you cut some of your expenses to make sure that you don't end up out on the street?" It is unfortunate, but for too many people, it takes something drastic like a bankruptcy before they get motivated to do something about their finances.

Joseph was suddenly propelled from his comfort and he had to do something. What he did showed that he had character. He clung to the dream that God had given him and he hung on to the word of God. That is why he was able to go from the pit to the throne, from slavery to the dream. His character caused him to rise in every circumstance and to rise above every obstacle. That is why we need the Word of God. We need to confess it and develop it in our lives.

If you look up the word "motivation" in the dictionary, it is defined as to incite into movement or an action; an idea, a need, an emotion that provokes us to action. God motivates us by fear and by reward. The world uses some of the same techniques. In some cases, people are motivated by fear to get saved. They don't want to go to hell and burn in fire. For others, it is the reward that draws them to salvation. They see that if they are born again, they will be blessed. Either way, you are still saved. The motivation gets us moving in the right direction.

Joseph was motivated by his desire to fulfill a dream. If you're trying to get motivated, you need to get desire for whatever your dream is. Meditate on that dream and begin to see that dream and think about the reward. If you feel some fear about it, let that become a motivation to drive you toward the fulfillment of the dream. Just keep yourself moving forward.

Joseph was motivated to live right spiritually, which motivated him to change areas of his soul so that character was developed that could control his flesh and make it obedient to the dream.

CHAPTER 7:

Fear of Change

The reason that we seek comfort is because of fear. We always want comfort, enough to eat, good clothes, a nice place to live, a good car to drive. But the underlying desire is for security. We want to know that things are not going to change.

The problem is that there is no security on the face of the earth except our security in Christ Jesus. You can't be secure in your job. You can't be secure in the world's economy. You can't be secure in any area. You don't know what tomorrow holds.

So we seek comfort in order not to have to face the unknowns and uncertainties. It is interesting that people can become comfortable anywhere. You can get comfortable with living in a cardboard box and eating out of a dumpster behind McDonald's. You can get comfortable because, even if it isn't that great of a life, at least you know what to expect. Most people prefer a hell that they are familiar with than a paradise that they haven't seen. Your fear hinders you.

God calls us to a position of faith, however, not fear. The security that we think we have is illusory. Change is good. We should be constantly growing and changing. That means that we have to move further than where we are. We can't seek comfort and we can't seek security.

Once you understand the process of wealth, you realize that you could lose everything and get it all back again because you know how the system works and you know that you will continue to gain wealth. Once you get to that point, you'll never worry or be in fear again. That is the place from which God wants us to operate. He does not want us in fear. When you live in fear, your wealth controls you. You serve it, rather than having it serve you. Jesus said it this way:

> *No one can serve two masters; for either he will hate the one and love the other, or else he will be loyal to the one and despise the other. You cannot serve God and mammon* (Matthew 6:24).

To put God's plan for your life in its simplest form, He wants you to get a job, work for seed, invest into the Kingdom of God and invest into the earth. He will cause whatever your hands touch to prosper and as soon as your investment in the earth begins to produce a dividend that exceeds your expense level, then money is working for you. When money is working for you, you can work for God. You cannot serve God effectively if all of your energy is devoted to working for money.

Jesus continued by focusing on worry:

> *Therefore I say to you, do not worry about your life, what you will eat or what you will drink; nor about your body, what you will put on. Is not life more than food and the body more than clothing? Look at the birds of the air, for they neither sow nor reap nor gather into barns; yet your heavenly Father feeds them. Are you not of more value than they? Which of you by worrying can add one cubit to his stature? So why do you worry about clothing? Consider the lilies of the field, how they grow; they neither toil nor spin, and yet I say to you that even Solomon in all his glory was not arrayed like one of these. Now if God so clothes the grass of the field, which today is, and tomorrow is thrown into the oven, will He not much more clothe you, O you of little faith? Therefore do not worry, saying, "What shall we eat?" or "What shall we drink?" or "What shall we wear?" For after all these things the Gentiles seek. For your heavenly Father knows that you need all these things* (Matthew 6:25-32).

Jesus said that worrying will do nothing but shorten your life. Your continued worrying is doing you no good at all. It is doing you harm. It is hurting your physical life and health. It is confusing and damaging to your mind. You're not able to think about what you could be doing and

the opportunities that are available because you're worrying about what's going to happen.

There is a remedy for worry. Jesus gives it in the next
verse:

> *But seek first the kingdom of God and His*
> *righteousness, and all these things shall be added*
> *to you* (Matthew 6:33).

Seeking the Kingdom of God means more than just
reading this book. We've been given the position or the
ministry of reconciliation. We saw earlier that this means
not only to reconcile people, but to reconcile all things, reconcile them to the Kingdom of God. It means that we've
been given the responsibility to win the lost through the
blood of Jesus. It also means we've been given the responsibility to take the wealth of the wicked and bring it into the
Kingdom of God. We are to reconcile all things.

When we seek the Kingdom of God, we become doers
of the Word and not hearers only. Jesus said that if we will
do this, then all those other things — food, clothing, shelter,
wealth—will come to us.

Here is where many people miss the point, however.
They think that if they are just sitting around seeking God
and reading the Bible twenty hours a day, then they are
seeking the Kingdom and they won't have to do anything
else. I see it often in Christians. Someone cries out, "I'm
going to get ahold of God. I'm praying twenty hours a day
in my cabin in the woods. I'm seeking God. I'm going to

pray at the horns of the altar and weep and cry and beg and I'm going to get God to move on my behalf and He's going to give me wealth and health."

At the same time, God is saying, "Why don't you just start eating right? Get a job. Then you'll have some money. Invest it and see what happens."

Seeking the Kingdom of God is not isolating yourself from the world. It is entering into the ministry of reconciling the earth to Him. It means doing the Word. Faith without works is dead.

There is no security outside of the knowledge of Christ.

There is no security outside of the knowledge of Christ. Think about how many people in the Old Testament had to move from their comfort to face their fears because God commanded them to move. Abraham had to leave his country and his family, all of his security. God didn't even tell him where he was going. His instruction was just to go to a "land that I will show you." That's pretty vague. But Abraham trusted God and he moved, therefore he received the promises.

David left the security and comfort of taking care of his sheep to go and face a giant. He gained a kingdom. Jacob left his home to go to a distant land where he knew no one and had nothing. He came back as one of the richest men in the world.

God always leads us out of our comfort to face our fears. And when we face our fears, we can come into faith and believe God and then we see His promises fulfilled in our lives.

Comfort and fear of change is what stops most people. There is a story about a mountain in Switzerland. It can be climbed in one day up and one day back. About halfway up the mountain, there is a cabin where climbers can rest with a warm fire and a good meal.

People prepare and train for the climb. They train and exercise, walking and climbing, to get used to the lower oxygen levels at the high elevation. They learn to repel and run ropes and drive spikes and use all of the gear that they will need for the climb. They make sure that they have the right clothing.

The day finally comes for the climb and they join a team at the base of the mountain. Together, they start an early morning climb. It is a rugged, exhausting climb. Halfway through the day, they arrive at the cabin. There is a warm fire and good food. They take off their gear and relax on a soft couch. The view is wonderful and life is great. They get comfortable.

Then the time comes to continue. Inevitably, there are only a few who put all of their gear back on and continue up the mountain. The others sit around the fire, talking and singing and eating. They say goodbye to their companions and tell them that they will join them tomorrow for the trip down.

About four o'clock in the afternoon, just as the sun drops behind the mountain, it suddenly grows quiet in the cabin. One by one, those who stayed behind drift to the telescope where they can see the top of the mountain or they pull out binoculars and look up at their friends who are just about to arrive at the peak, just about to accomplish the goal, nearly at the completion of the climb.

In the silence, each begins to wonder what it would be like to be up there. They begin to consider the wisdom of choosing comfort over the goal. But by then, it is too late to go. All they can do is watch others succeed who decided to leave the comfort of the cabin behind.

Too many Christians do the same thing in their lives. They prepare through schooling and education. They learn from their experiences. They learn the Word. They study and meditate on how to become successful. They confess the Word. Then they start out on the road to success.

> The best way to make tomorrow better is to do something today that's going to improve it.

Then they find a place that is comfortable. It's been a tough road so they tell themselves that they need to rest a little. And they never move any further. At the end of their lives, they will listen while Jesus says to others, "Well done, good and faithful servant." Then when it is their turn, all they will hear is, "Did you run the race? Did you do all that you could? Did you pursue the dream that I gave you?" And they will have the regrets of having chosen comfort.

Napoleon Hill said, "Whatever the mind of man can conceive and believe, it can achieve." The apostle Paul said it this way. "I can do all things through Christ who strengthens me" (Philippians 4:13). Jesus said, "All things are possible to him who believes" (Matthew 9:23).

The best way to manage your future is to begin to create it today. The best way to make tomorrow better is to do something today that's going to improve it. Otherwise, tomorrow's going to be just like today. When you step out of the boat, you are with Jesus. When you stay in the boat, all you've got is bad weather and more disciples.

Let's go to the top. Let's run our race. Your past is not your future. Too many people believe that their past and the future are the same, that what they have already lived is exactly what they will live. But that's not God's plan. He said to forget the past. He said to forget those things that are past and press on to the high calling. That does not mean staying where you are. It means getting out of your comfort zone and moving forward.

Joseph and the Famine

Joseph was a man who was not afraid to try something different. He definitely thought outside the box. He did not do things just because everyone else thought it was the way it should be done. We see an important lesson in one incident in particular.

As Joseph's father, Jacob, also called Israel, was advancing in years, Joseph took his two sons to be blessed by their grandfather. This was a common practice in the Old Testament. The patriarch of the family would lay his hands on the children and pronounce a blessing over them.

Traditionally, the firstborn son received twice as much

inheritance as the others and so it was always assumed that he should have the greatest part of the blessing as well. It was customary for the patriarch to place his right hand on the oldest son and his left hand on the other. That was how Joseph presented his sons to his father. Manasseh was the firstborn, so Joseph put him on the left of his brother, Ephraim, so that Jacob's right hand would naturally rest on his head.

But when Jacob reached out to bless the two boys, he did something interesting.

> *Then Israel stretched out his right hand and laid it on Ephraim's head, who was the younger, and his left hand on Manasseh's head, guiding his hands knowingly, for Manasseh was the firstborn* (Genesis 48:14).

He switched hands. He broke tradition. He did something that was out of the norm. Joseph tried to stop him, but Jacob insisted.

> *Now when Joseph saw that his father laid his right hand on the head of Ephraim, it displeased him; so he took hold of his father's hand to remove it from Ephraim's head to Manasseh's head. And Joseph said to his father, "Not so, my father, for this one is the firstborn; put your right hand on his head."*
>
> *But his father refused and said, "I know, my*

*son, I know. He also shall become a people, and he
also shall be great; but truly his younger brother
shall be greater than he, and his descendants
shall become a multitude of nations"* (Genesis
48:17-19).

The lesson here is that God looks at the heart, not at
the lineage. If you think that you cannot succeed because
you are poor and your family has always been poor, then
you have not understood how God works. He always gives
preference to those who are willing to do things His way,
regardless of where they start.

We see this many times in Scripture. Ephraim and Manasseh were not the first and would not be the last examples
of it. Jacob himself was not the firstborn. To all appear-
ances, his brother Esau should have gotten the inheritance
and the blessing. But Esau traded it away. Jacob was willing and so God blessed him instead of the firstborn.

Cain was the firstborn, but God gave preference to the
offering of his brother, Abel. The reason was because of
the attitude that Abel had.

*And in the process of time it came to pass
that Cain brought an offering of the fruit of the
ground to the LORD. Abel also brought of the
firstborn of his flock and of their fat. And the LORD
respected Abel and his offering* (Genesis 4:3-4).

The difference was that Abel brought the best, the firstborn, the fat portion. He honored God with the best that he had. Cain just brought whatever.

On a greater scale, Adam was to be the ruler of the earth. But he lost it through sin. The inheritance passed to the second Adam, to Jesus Christ, who came in obedience and did the will of the Father.

God does not give preference to the one we think He should. He seems to favor the second, for no other reason than the attitude of the heart. Even the nation of Israel illustrates this. They were the chosen people of God, given an exalted position in the world, the favored of God. It was through them that the Messiah was born into this world.

He wants to make you first, raise you to the top and bring you great prosperity.

The problem was that God intended that they use that position of favor to be a blessing to the world. Instead, they became proud of it and began to avoid the rest of the world. When the Messiah came, they completely rejected Him. John 1:10 tells us that Jesus came to His own and His own didn't receive Him. As a result, God rejected them and went to the ones who would receive. God responds to "whosoever will"—whosoever will respond to Him, whosoever will obey Him, whosoever will step out and start to move forward in reconciling the earth to His Kingdom.

You have been sent out as sheep among wolves. It's not normal for sheep to overcome wolves, but that is exactly what God has in mind. The world system may try to convince you that you are not the appropriate one to succeed, but that isn't God's way of doing things. He wants to make you first, raise you to the top and bring you great prosperity.

The Secret of Wealth

It is amazing just how simple Joseph's success was when we consider what he did. He used basic common sense business practices and in the end, he controlled all of the wealth of Egypt. In Genesis 41, we read of a dream that Pharaoh had that he couldn't understand. Joseph was brought to him and explained that God was giving him a warning. There would be seven years of great abundance followed by seven years of severe famine.

As a result, Joseph was put in charge of preparing for the famine. How he handled the situation shows us the basic secret of wealth. During the years of abundance, while everything was cheap, he bought everything he could.

> *So he gathered up all the food of the seven years which were in the land of Egypt, and laid up the food in the cities; he laid up in every city the food of the fields which surrounded them. Joseph gathered very much grain, as the sand of the sea, until he stopped counting, for it was immeasurable* (Genesis 41:48-49).

When the years of famine came, Joseph was prepared for it. As the food supply failed, Joseph began to sell off what he had stored up during the years of plenty. He kept selling until there was no money left in Egypt. Joseph had it all.

> *And Joseph gathered up all the money that was found in the land of Egypt and in the land of Canaan, for the grain which they bought; and Joseph brought the money into Pharaoh's house* (Genesis 47:14).

After the money failed, Joseph began to barter. People agreed to trade their livestock for food. Before long, Joseph owned all the livestock in the land. The next year, they traded their land and before long, Joseph owned all the land.

Christians are selling themselves short to the world.

You can buy low when there's too much and then, when there's not enough, sell high. It is the secret of wealth. If you do that, wealth cannot elude you. The problem is that we buy high and sell low and then wonder why we stay in poverty.

There are so many things in life to which you can apply this principle, if you will just look around at the opportunities. If you sell something for one dollar more than you paid for it, you've made a profit. That was all Joseph did.

Christians are selling themselves short to the world. Jesus paid a complete price to buy us out of poverty and to put us into prosperity. He paid the price so that you don't have to be sick or broke. It doesn't matter where you started. God intends success for you.

For you see your calling, brethren, that not many wise according to the flesh, not many mighty, not many noble, are called. But God has chosen the foolish things of the world to put to shame the wise, and God has chosen the weak things of the world to put to shame the things which are mighty; and the base things of the world and the things which are despised God has chosen, and the things which are not, to bring to nothing the things that are (1 Corinthians 1:26-28).

The word "foolish" means those who need help. God takes those who recognize that they can't do it on their own and brings them to success.

The "weak" are those who are naïve, laughable or average. God has called us out of average. He will take average people and make them great.

The "base" are an interesting group. This word, in Greek, refers to the comatose, the airheads. You may not think you have any brains at all, but God said that He would even take the comatose and airheads and elevate them.

God wants us to take poverty and make it nothing because we have gained wealth. He wants us to take sickness and make it nothing because we have gained health. He wants us to take grief and sorrow and make them nothing because we have gained joy. He wants us to take confusion and make it nothing because we have taken peace. He wants us to take every promise in His Word and use them to reconcile the earth to His Kingdom.

CHAPTER 8:

Investment—The Only
Way to Too Much

The world has figured out that if they invest their time and their lives into something, they will produce wealth. We all know people in the world who are very wealthy people. The problem is that they can't enjoy their wealth. They still have fear, worry, greed, lust, selfish ambition and all sorts of things that torment them.

When we got born again, we left that system behind and joined a new system. God wants us to have too much, but He wants us to have it with joy and peace and health and without worry. We just have to do it His way.

The principle of investment is not just a part of the world's system. It is a principle that God has given us. Unfortunately, too many Christians have ignored it. We've been sitting around, waiting for God to drop wealth in our laps. That isn't how He does it. You have to invest. God himself invested in the earth:

> *For God so loved the world that He gave*
> *His only begotten Son, that whoever believes in*

Him should not perish but have everlasting life (John 3:16).

We've all heard this verse hundreds of times. For those who grew up in church, it was probably the first verse that you memorized. Most Christians can quote it. What I want you to take note of right now is the first part. God so loved the world that He gave.

> **God wants us to have too much, but He wants us to have it with joy and peace and health and without worry.**

What God did was to invest in the earth. The earth had been lost to the enemy. When Adam sinned, he virtually turned the earth over to the enemy. So God said, "What needs to happen now is that I will invest something so that I can reap a harvest."

God sent His Son. Jesus, the Word, became flesh. Jesus became the seed that God planted in the earth. Jesus was planted as an investment.

Jesus said that unless a seed falls to the ground and dies, it cannot produce (John 12:24). He died, was buried and rose from the grave and through Him, all of mankind can be redeemed. God sowed one seed and He's reaped millions as a result. In fact, He's still reaping a harvest from that one seed. He paid the supreme price, but He has gained a great, great value in return.

God reaped from His sowing. This principle is the foundation of everything in life. The idea of sowing and reaping has been there from the beginning and it will not go away. God told Noah that it was an eternal principle.

> *While the earth remains,*
> *Seedtime and harvest,*
> *Cold and heat,*
> *Winter and summer,*
> *And day and night*
> *Shall not cease.*
> (Genesis 8:22)

As long as the earth endures, we will have these things. Seedtime and harvest will be with us. It's how everything works.

Now let's take that understanding into our world. Seedtime is when you plant. Seedtime is investment. Harvest is when you reap from what you have planted.

Jesus became the seed that God planted in the earth.

Harvest is the dividend. You cannot gain too much without investment. It just won't work any other way.

God requires four basic investments of us if we want to have too much. We need to make sure that we invest in all four.

1. Invest Yourself

The first thing that God requires is that you invest yourself into His Kingdom. You have to leave that old life and enter into a new life. He wants you to become born of the

Spirit so that you become a part of His Kingdom. He is the Father and He doesn't want anyone to perish. It is a choice that you have to make. God has prepared a place for those who won't accept Him. You do have a choice.

If you will sow yourself into salvation and receive Jesus as your Savior, you become born again. According to the principle of sowing and harvest, that means that you have to reap something from your investment. There has to be a harvest. We find that harvest described in Romans.

> *Therefore we were buried with Him through baptism into death, that just as Christ was raised from the dead by the glory of the Father, even so we also should walk in newness of life. For if we have been united together in the likeness of His death, certainly we also shall be in the likeness of His resurrection, knowing this, that our old man was crucified with Him, that the body of sin might be done away with, that we should no longer be slaves of sin* (Romans 6:4-6).

There are several things there that are part of your harvest. You reap newness of life. You reap forgiveness of all of your sin—past, present and future. You reap a robe of righteousness that now covers you and places you in right standing with God. You are covered by the blood of Jesus and you are brand new.

It's kind of like my grandson. When he was about four years old, we took him on a little trip in an airplane and he didn't like it. He didn't want to fly anymore. When we got to the plane for the return trip, he said, "Grandpa, I already done that." Well, when it comes to death, we can say, "I already done that."

We've reaped life and we don't have to die anymore. We reap forgiveness, life, grace and righteousness. Our investment is paying tremendous eternal dividends.

2. Invest Your Tithe

The second area of investment that God expects from us is the tithe. In some ways, it is a matter of training. When you raise children, one of the earliest things that you want them to learn is obedience. There is a

> **Tithing is about obedience. It's not a matter of whether you like it or not.**

process that we go through to get them to understand the importance of obedience.

When you were born again, you were just a baby, and God had to do some training. He said, "Wherever your treasure is, there also is your heart" (Matthew 6:21). He said in Malachi, "Do this and test Me and see if this doesn't work." In other words, "Obey."

Tithing is about obedience. It's not a matter of whether you like it or not. He didn't ask you if you liked it. He just asked you if you would do it. If you will do it, it's one of the key steps to too much.

When you capture a child's heart, you can direct his life. If you never capture your child's heart, you will never direct his life. The same is true with you. If God can capture your heart, He can direct your life. That's why He wants what is very close to us. He knew that if He could get what is close to us, He would capture our hearts. Then we would obey Him and our hearts would begin to enter His Kingdom.

That is why He asks for the tithe. If you put your treasure into the Kingdom, then your heart will be there also. If your heart is there, then God can direct your life. If God can direct your life, then He can bring blessing to you.

3. Invest Your Offering

God also wants you to grow in love. That's where He is trying to bring your heart. Step 3 is the investment of your offering because your offering is a measurement of love. You can give it or not give it. The tithe, God requires, but the offering is your choice. It is a measurement of love.

If you have just enough to get by, it's hard to give an offering. You can't put much in. God wants us to have so much that when we give an offering, we do so joyfully and cheerfully. If you give and because you gave, your kids won't get shoes, that's kind of a drag. It's hard to give.

I can remember when I was in a situation where we didn't have enough money to pay the bills at the end of the month, so I sowed the little bit of money I did have. I gave an offering. I wasn't going to be able to pay the bills anyway, so I sowed in the famine. As a result, God met my need at the end of the month. He will do that, so don't misunderstand what I'm saying, but He is still looking for the cheerful giver.

Paul had been in Corinth. They were planning to give an offering. This was not their tithe. They were going to give an offering to a mission for the church in Jerusalem that was in need at the time. So Paul appealed to those who had too much to get them to give to some who had too little. He told them that he was going to send someone to collect the offering and he told them that they should be cheerful about giving it.

The offering should be according to your heart.

> *So let each one give as he purposes in his heart, not grudgingly or of necessity; for God loves a cheerful giver* (2 Corinthians 9:7).

There are some who point to that verse as proof that they don't need to tithe, that Paul said to give according to what you can give. But this is not the tithe. This is an offering that Paul was referring to. The offering should be according to your heart. It is a measure of love. It shows that you have a heart for the Kingdom of God. God views the heart.

Romans 6:14 tells us that we are not under the law, but under grace. God has brought you into a position of grace. He wants you to operate in what Jesus has already done for you, not in a position of the law. He wants you to give because you love His Kingdom, not because somebody's requiring it of you. It is a measurement of your heart. If your offering is a dollar, but you're cheerful about it, then God's excited, too.

Paul says to be a cheerful giver. But just before that verse, we again see the idea of sowing. The offering is an investment and there is a harvest connected to it.

> *But this I say: He who sows sparingly will also reap sparingly, and he who sows bountifully will also reap bountifully* (2 Corinthians 9:6).

In other words, you are not to give grudgingly because it is really one of your investments. You should be excited about it. You give out of love for the Kingdom and you give because you know that it will bring a harvest that will enable you to give even more. Your offering has the power to produce something.

Malachi 3:10-12 gives us a good picture of just what it is that this investment produces. The tithes cause God to rebuke the devourer so that he cannot take our possessions. The offerings open the windows of heaven so that a blessing is poured out.

What I want you to see is that the blessing is not money being poured into your lap. It is a blessing that causes growth and multiplication in your investments in the earth. This brings us to the next area.

4. Invest in the Earth

Blessing, the way that it is pictured in Malachi and other places in the Old Testament, has the image of rain falling on crops and causing them to grow. It is not money that God manufactures to rain down on you. If there is nothing planted, then the blessing has nothing to fall on.

This is the area that so many don't understand. God wants us to invest in all four of these areas. First, we invest in ourselves. We reap the benefits of forgiveness and eternal life.

Next, He wants us to invest in the tithe. That works like an insurance policy. When we tithe, God rebukes the devourer and the enemy can no longer touch our stuff. God protects it.

The third investment is in the offering, which is a measurement of our love for the Kingdom of God. It gets our hearts deeper and deeper into the Kingdom so that God has greater control over our lives and the Holy Spirit can steer us in the right direction more effectively. Then the offering has the power to multiply in our lives.

> **If you withhold your tithe, the enemy will have an open door to steal from you.**

Fourth, we have to plant something in the earth. There has to be some sort of investment that God can multiply. That is the point at which we reclaim the earth.

If you withhold, you will never grow. People come into the church and sit in a back corner. They want to hear a little and then go their way. But they're not willing to invest themselves in the Kingdom. When you are unwilling to invest yourself, the Word has no power in you and, as a result, you never grow. You'll be the same twenty years from now as you are today. If you withhold yourself, you'll never grow.

If you withhold your tithe, the enemy will have an open door to steal from you. It will seem that you're never getting anywhere because as soon as you get a little ahead, something happens and you lose it all.

If you withhold your offering, then you will not see the multiplication in your life that comes from the blessing being poured out. If you withhold your offering, your love will not be for the work of God.

If you withhold your investment in the earth—business, real estate or whatever it might be—you will not experience increase. God has to have something to bless.

To Save that Which Was Lost

Everything in the Bible is about giving. The Word will always work through your giving. The Word won't work in your marriage until you're able to give yourself to your mate. The Word won't work in a relationship until you're able to give love to someone else. It's not about expecting love. It's about giving love. Everything is about giving and the Word will only work through giving.

In Luke 19, we find Jesus passing through Jericho. Jesus is the Word of God. Jericho was the first fruits of the Promised Land when Israel first entered in. It was the first city that Joshua captured. God demanded all of it for Himself. After that, they got to keep the spoils of their victories, but Jericho belonged to God. It was the tithe. So Jesus, the

Word, was passing through the first fruits of the Promised Land.

In Jericho, there was a man named Zacchaeus who was a chief tax collector and he was very rich. He was also very short. He wanted to see Jesus but he couldn't get through to the front of the crowd and he couldn't see over other people.

Now, don't you think that if he was really rich and looked really rich, that the poor would have stepped aside for him? That is how it works. If he really wanted to, he could have been in the front. But Zacchaeus wasn't sure he wanted to be seen by the Word. He just wanted to see the Word, but not be seen himself.

He ran ahead of the crowd and climbed up into a sycamore tree so that he could see Jesus as He passed by. But he got a surprise. When Jesus got there, he walked right over to the tree.

> And when Jesus came to the place, He looked up and saw him, and said to him, "Zacchaeus, make haste and come down, for today I must stay at your house" (Luke 19:5).

This is a remarkable turn of events. Jesus, the Word, stopped and called out to a tax collector, one of the most despised men in society. There are some imperatives in Jesus' words. "Make haste" means that Zacchaeus was commanded to receive the Word—today. Not later, but today. The Word found him and said, "Zacchaeus, there is something that's going to happen that you have to have and you have to have it right now. I see your heart. It is committed. It is convicted of your past. That's why you're hiding from the Word."

If he had been just some old sinner who stumbled out in front of the crowd, it wouldn't have mattered to Jesus. But because Zacchaeus was convicted of the Word, he was trying to hide from it. The conviction was there and Jesus said, "It's imperative. You have to receive this Word today. I'm going to be at your house and stay today."

When the Word of God is moving you, that is the time to respond. Don't hide from it. Act immediately. The wonderful thing is that Zacchaeus did respond. He had dinner with Jesus and he repented of everything he had ever done. He got saved. In verse 9, Jesus said, "Today salvation has come to this house." That is the reconciliation of bringing people into the Kingdom.

Then Jesus made an interesting statement:

> *"For the Son of Man has come to seek and to save that which was lost"* (Luke 19:10).

This is interesting because He says that He came to save "that" which was lost, not just "those" who were lost. He came to claim lost souls, but He also came to reclaim all of the lost wealth and all of creation.

It is in this context that Jesus told the Parable of the Minas that we talked about earlier. He described the nobleman who called together ten servants and gave each a mina and then he left. When he returned, he called them in to see "how much every man had gained by trading" (verse 15). He expected them to conduct business, to invest. Trading means to buy low and sell high.

The first had multiplied his mina to ten. The second had increased to five. The nobleman commended both of them and called them "good and faithful" servants. The third didn't do anything with his and he was chastised for not doing business.

In this parable, Jesus spoke directly about the day that He would return. There are many who are sitting around waiting for the Second Coming. They are hoping that it will happen before they have to pay their bills again. Many have sold their homes and property because they didn't see any point in working if the return of Jesus is so close.

God seems to think that investment is important.

It is interesting that Jesus doesn't even hint at the possibility that when He returns, He will ask people, "Did you sell all that you had so that you would be ready for My return? Did you quit your job and stop working so that you could wait without any distractions?" He didn't ask those kinds of questions. He asked His servants if they had been trading. Had they been investing and reclaiming the wealth of the earth? Those who did not are called "wicked." God seems to think that investment is important.

CHAPTER 9:

Slaying the Giant

No one just walks into success overnight. It is a process of growth and development. If you are not there by tomorrow, don't quit. Keep developing the character of a successful person in yourself and you will be a successful person.

Many are dealing with "just enough." You have enough at the end of the month. You can go to the movies, drive your car a little extra, and maybe buy some shoes or odds and ends. You pay your bills and you've got a little bit left over. But it's not enough.

Other people are lacking. They don't have quite enough. They can't get things that they would like to have. They can't go out. They are right on the edge.

Then there are others who are in poverty. Poverty means that you don't even have enough to meet your basic needs. You don't know how you're going to make it through the end of the month. You're struggling and you're living in a sense of poverty.

All three of these areas are giants in the body of Christ.

Whichever one you are facing probably seems bigger than you can overcome. You don't know how to overcome.

Keep developing the character of a successful person in yourself and you will be a successful person.

Some have learned to defeat those giants, but not many. God desires that we seek prosperity for the sake of the house of the Lord. He wants us to share in all of the good things. That means that every Christian should be prospering and blessed so that they can be a blessing in every situation. But not all are. It isn't until you do something that it actually changes. You know that you should invest, but you just don't know how.

So we have some giants. You determine the caliber of a person by the amount of opposition that it takes to discourage him, by the size of the obstacle or the amount of opposition that it takes to stop him. What does it take to stop you? You need to evaluate that and then change it. There will be some opposition to your dreams. You have to overcome it.

God promised us a soft and safe landing. He didn't promise us a calm passage. There are some storms in life. He would never use the words "more than a conqueror" if there were not some things that need to be conquered. There are some giants to overcome.

David was a man who had obstacles to overcome. We all know the story of how he confronted and defeated Goliath. He acted for the sake of his nation, Israel, for the sake

of his family and for the reward for himself. He was motivated on all three levels. A higher cause than himself drove
him to success.

It is important to recognize
that David didn't just walk out
and kill a giant. He had some
previous experience that prepared him for that moment.
King Saul didn't think that such

> **God promised us a soft
> and safe landing. He
> didn't promise us a calm
> passage.**

a young man could face a seasoned veteran like Goliath.
But David recounted his past victories.

> *But David said to Saul, "Your servant used
> to keep his father's sheep, and when a lion or a
> bear came and took a lamb out of the flock, I went
> out after it and struck it, and delivered the lamb
> from its mouth; and when it arose against me, I
> caught it by its beard, and struck and killed it.
> Your servant has killed both lion and bear; and
> this uncircumcised Philistine will be like one of
> them, seeing he has defied the armies of the living
> God"* (1 Samuel 17:34-36).

This wasn't completely new ground for David. He had
already killed a bear and a lion. In other words, he had to
kill a couple of smaller things before he took on the larger
thing.

You can't just destroy poverty in your life overnight.
You have to take some territory on the way to having too

much. Despise not small beginnings. If you're faithful in the little, God will make you a ruler over much. The key is beginning. You might be thinking about it, talking about it. You're going to invest someday. But it's kind of like a race: If you don't start running, you'll never finish.

David started with a bear. I have some experience with bears. Growing up, I lived in the country, so I ran into bears occasionally. When you startle a bear, he figures that he's in for a battle, so what he does is stand up as tall as he can to frighten you with his size. Typically, that is how they act. They want to impress you with how big and powerful they are.

If you're faithful in the little, God will make you a ruler over much.

They don't normally attack you.

I ran into a particular bear one day when I was about fifteen years old. I was heading into the woods to cut some pulp. It was about a mile and a half back to where I was working. It was early in the morning and I had my Mc-Cullough chain saw, my oil can and my gas can and I was walking in the dark. The sun was just barely high enough to start lighting the sky. I could just see silhouettes as I walked.

I came to a creek and just across on the other side, there was a raspberry patch. I heard something and then, it stood up where I could see its silhouette—a huge black bear.

I set down my gas can and said, "McCullough, don't fail me now." I pulled it twice and it fired up. The noise scared the bear off, but for the rest of the summer, that bear ate my lunch. I would hide it in trees, but he still found it and shook the tree until it came down. I was just glad that he wasn't eating me.

David killed a bear first. He learned that the menacing appearance of the bear was not something that should cause him to run. He learned to face the bear squarely and defeat it. It was an easy target to aim at. That was a good beginning.

But then he had to face a lion. The lion attacks in a different way from the bear. He runs straight at you. Now, David had a moving target. It was more difficult and more dangerous than the bear. But because David had the experience with the bear, he was ready for the lion.

By the time David faced Goliath, he had gotten in some practice. He wasn't just jumping into the battle without some training. He worked his way up to that moment and he was ready.

The Bear of Debt

When we looked at the Parable of the Sower in Mark 4, we saw the different things that cause the Word to fail in our lives. With the first, the enemy stole it. With the second, it had no root and couldn't survive opposition. The third scenario is very specific. It describes ground that was unfruitful because the cares of this world and the deceitfulness of riches and the desire for other things enter in and choke the Word.

What are the cares of the world? I believe they are identified by debt. Debt is one of the things that you worry about. You fret over it because you have to make sure that you have enough money at the end of the month. You have to have just enough to make all the payments.

Earlier we defined what debt is. You need to clearly understand this. Debt is when you owe more on something than you can sell it for. If you can sell it for more than you paid for it, then it is an asset. When I understood this, I started collecting different things that would increase in value. They are assets. Some of them will go to my grand-

Debt is something that eats up your ability to invest in the earth.

children. If I can buy a coin today that was minted in the 1800s for $200, it may be worth enough by the time my grand-children are out of high school to pay for their college. That is an asset.

The kind of debt that is a problem is debt that you can't get rid of by selling the thing. Credit cards are debt. It is just money that you owe, not an asset that can bring you money. Debt is something that eats up your ability to invest in the earth. All of your seed for investment is used to pay the interest on your debt. You are financing the world with the interest that you pay.

I've experienced how much debt can limit you. There was a time when my wife, Maureen, and I had $15 to our name, no car and a lot of debt. We decided to get out of debt. It took some effort, but we did it.

I took two jobs. Then I added another one because two wasn't doing it. This is not impossible for most people. The average person wastes thirty-nine hours a week. If you count eight hours a night of sleep, time that you spend with your spouse, time with your children, time that you work your regular job and add them all together, there is an average of thirty-nine hours a week available to you for other jobs.

That was how we got out of debt. Nearly anyone can work an extra part-time job or two and use that money to pay off things like credit cards. Then you can set aside some money to invest. That's how you defeat debt.

Once you start investing, your money can multiply. If you set aside $5 a week, you could begin investing. Go down to a park and swap or go to garage sales and look for something that's broken that you can fix. Buy it for $5 and fix it up. If you do that every week for three months, you will have $60 invested. Then have your own garage sale and sell everything that you fixed up, painted, touched up and cleaned up for twice what you paid for it. Now you've got $120 to work with. Keep doing that and it won't be long before you have plenty of money to invest. In a matter of thirty-six months, if you just kept doubling your money every three months, you would have nearly $400,000. Anyone can do it.

I borrowed $16,000 and invested in some property with two other people. We had just enough for the down payment. It turned into $359,000 in two years and after three and a half years, the investment was worth over a million dollars.

David started out by killing a bear. Debt is a bear that you have to overcome. Until you do that, you will never have money to invest in anything and without investment, you will not gain too much.

The Lion of Want

After debt, the other thing in the Parable of the Sower that choked the Word into unfruitfulness was the desire for other things, the deceitfulness of riches. This is the desire to have what you can't afford. You need to kill the desire in you to have today what you can't afford so that one day, you can afford it.

That is how people get into debt in the first place. Credit says that you can buy now and pay later. And you will pay. If you buy a brand new car, the moment you drive it off the lot, you have just lost $5,000 to $8,000 or more.

If you have to have a new car, at least buy it smart. Decide what you can afford as a monthly payment. Push yourself to the limit. Buy a $20,000 car and say, "I want to pay it off in three years." The reason for this is that the car has a warranty for three years or 36,000 miles. It's completely covered from bumper to bumper. Now you don't have to worry about repairs on it. Then you make your payments.

Most people try to get the lowest payments that they can. They stretch the loan to sixty months, sometimes seventy-two, and end up paying an additional $10,000 to $15,000 in interest. Instead, press yourself to pay for the car in three years. By that time, it's paid for and it's got less than 36,000 miles on it. You can drive it and you have at least a $12,000 asset. If you want to trade for another new car, you have that much to put down on it and now your payments will be back around $200 a month.

It is not that complicated. You can learn the world's system and beat it. But you will have to bring your desires under control first.

The Giant of Poverty

David had the experience that he needed to prepare for the giant. He killed some smaller things first. That is how you defeat poverty, one enemy at a time. Kill the bear of debt and the lion of desire and you will

> **Kill the bear of debt and the lion of desire and you will be well on your way to overcoming poverty in your life.**

be well on your way to overcoming poverty in your life. You will be on your way to too much.

It takes work and it takes some planning, but you can do it. David, on his way out to face Goliath, picked up five stones. In theory, he only needed one shot. Goliath was a target that was too big to miss. But David planned ahead for the unexpected. He was ready. He would be facing a moving target that might be throwing things back at him. He was ready, just in case he missed.

The point is that you can do it. You can have too much. No matter where you are starting, you can take on each obstacle one at a time, learn how to do the things that you need to do and overcome. Despise not small beginnings. You have to start somewhere, but you do have to start.

CHAPTER 10:

Want To Versus Need To

Americans are caught in a web of want tos. All of our desires, all of our passion and all of our drive direct us toward what we want or feel like doing. Do what feels good. Live for today. Buy now, pay later. Want tos are associated with feelings. "I feel like this." "I feel like doing that."

This really affects nearly everyone today. In the fifties, America experienced great affluence. There was more money than there was product and people began to experience a level of abundance unlike anything in history. Out of the affluent fifties came a lot of different styles of music and different clothing and there was a new class of citizens that we really didn't have before—teenagers. Before the fifties, you were a child, then you were an adult. There was no category in between.

But in the fifties, we suddenly had teenagers. All of the media understood that there was affluence. They also understood that there was a dollar to be made through the sale of music, clothing, and so on. So they explored how to target teenagers. It was the Fabulous Fifties and it was all about having fun.

Many of us grew up in that era. By the time we got into college, it was the sixties. Everything was about rebellion against authority, rebellion against responsibility. It was about free love. It was all about doing what you want to do and going where you want to go, in the words of the song by the Mamas and the Papas. In the sixties, it was all about, "If it feels good, do it."

This attitude carried over into the seventies and became a part of the lifestyle of society. It became a pervasive attitude, a perception that is planted in most of our hearts today. We are compelled to do what we feel like doing, what we want to do.

Even in church, we're caught up in the want. People want to relax and enjoy the music and the sermon. They don't want to actually do anything to help, like volunteer to usher or work in the nursery or something. It's not what they feel like doing.

Clothing styles reflect the attitude of the culture. In the sixties, when the attitude was, "If it feels good, do it," we saw miniskirts and short shorts. By 2000, baggy clothes were in style. But we became a society that needed baggy clothes to cover up our obesity. "If it tastes good, eat it." This is just another form of doing what we feel like. We wear baseball caps because we don't feel like combing our hair. We have a new style called "get up in the morning and spray it." It's called "bed head." We have breath mints because we don't feel like brushing our teeth. We have fast food because we don't feel like cooking.

Clearly, I'm being a little facetious about this, but I want you to understand the point. Success in life is connected to doing what you need to do, not what you want to do. "Want to" is directly connected to "feel like." We will say, "I feel like a Coke," or "I feel like a brownie." "I feel like a cigarette." Have you ever felt like a carrot? We want to do what we feel like doing, not what we need to do.

When it gets bad, we say, "I need deliverance." But what you need is to quit doing what you want to do and start doing what you need to do.

> **Success in life is connected to doing what you need to do, not what you want to do.**

I go on a fishing trip every year with my son, Scot. Last year, we were in a boat, floating on the river, and enjoying the time. It began to drizzle a little, so I got out my poncho and I continued fishing. In fact, the fishing was good. It was a very enjoyable time. And I suddenly felt like a cigarette.

Now I haven't smoked in thirty-five years. I quit because I do what I need to, not what I want to. This is where the decision-making process comes in. If you want to be successful, you have to begin doing what you need to do, not what you want to do.

From Passion to Action

Eve didn't just happen to run into the serpent one day and get caught up in the temptation. The implication in the

Hebrew is that she constantly heard him. He came to her day after day, continually speaking to her. Faith works the same way. In the New Testament, it really says that faith comes by hearing and hearing. What you listen to over and over again, you will eventually believe. That is what happened to Eve. She just kept listening and the more she heard the serpants voice, the more likely she was to believe it.

What the serpent kept telling her was that she should look at the tree of the knowledge of good and evil. He played on her desire.

> So when the woman saw that the tree was good for food, that it was pleasant to the eyes, and a tree desirable to make one wise, she took of its fruit and ate. She also gave to her husband with her, and he ate (Genesis 3:6).

Eve knew that she wasn't supposed to eat the fruit. She knew that it would not be a good thing for her life. God told her very plainly not to eat of that tree. Everything else was available to her. She understood that. But she continued to hear something contrary to what she knew and she began to see that the tree was desirable.

Desire creates passion. Passion creates a drive or a motivation to do or to bring out the action. You can use this positively or you can use it negatively. Eve chose to allow desire to rise and as it did, it created a passion in her that caused her to choose what she wanted to do, not what she needed to do.

This is what happens when we see crimes of passion. Road rage happens because someone allows feelings to cause desire, which drives passion and then the action becomes a violent outburst that was what the person felt like doing, not what he needed to do. This is what happens in marriage so often. Instead of doing what they need to do, which is love each other, couples start allowing their feelings to draw them away from their commitments. If the feelings are indulged for long enough, they create desire, then passion, and the result is a divorce.

This is what happened to Cain. God came right to him and said, "You didn't give the right offering, but I'll give you another chance. Sin is crouching at your door. Choose wisely." But Cain did what he wanted to do, not what he needed to do. If he would have repented and done the right thing, his life would have been different.

When it comes to tithes and offerings, how many people give God what they want to, rather than what they need to? You need a big harvest, but you are not willing to give a big seed. You should be active in serving in some capacity, but you don't feel "led."

If you can turn this trend around in your life, you will completely stop procrastinating. You'll stop putting things off. I can't procrastinate. Sometimes my wife wishes that I would. But I am driven to do what I need to do, not what I want to do.

This is a decision that you make on a daily basis. If you will continually make decisions based on doing what you need to do before you do what you want to do, you will have success. It will come to you no matter what.

Noah is a good example. He was 360 years old. At that age, he probably thought that it was time to relax a little, just kick back in the recliner and take it easy. But God came to him and said, "I want you to build a big boat and I want you to do it right here in the middle of the desert."

Now, Noah would have to go all the way to the hills of Lebanon, cut down huge trees, hew the trees and drag them down to the desert from the mountains in order to build a boat in the desert. And all of that would be to protect himself from something that had never happened before in history—rain.

But Noah did what he needed to do in obedience to the Word, not what he wanted to do. As a result, he saved all life on this planet.

Train Up a Child

Proverbs talks about training your children. There are many references, but one in particular, we are familiar with.

Train up a child in the way he should go,
And when he is old he will not depart from it
(Proverbs 22:6).

What does it mean to train a child? What is the process? We know that there are certain things that we want to see in them. We want them to love people and love and respect their parents. But how do we do that?

Training is a matter of creating habits that they will not depart from. Think about what kind of habits you train in children. Do you train them to do their want tos first or do you train them to do their need tos? If you don't train them, kids will always choose want to first. You can go to any mall and watch young kids and how they behave and it is obvious that a great many parents haven't done any training at all. Kids are indulging in their want tos without any regard for their need tos.

We are supposed to train children to do what they need to do before they do what they want to do. You need to train your children to brush their teeth and comb their hair. Train them that they need to clean their room and pick up their toys before they play video games. If you let them play first, then you're training them to do want tos first.

I see parents all the time who say that their teenager doesn't want to come to church, so they left him home. It is a matter of training. When my kids didn't want to go to church, they went anyway, because they needed to. "You will go to church. We are not discussing it. You are the child and you will go. When you're an adult, then you can decide."

I wrestle with this as a grandparent. As a parent, I trained my sons to do what they needed to do first. As a grandparent, however, I want to give my grandchildren what they want. I sometimes have to bite my tongue. But it is vital to a child's development that he learn this at an early age. I want them to be blessed and to be happy. I want them to love their grandpa. But they need to be trained. If they go into adulthood doing their want tos before their need tos, they won't be able to hold a job for very long. They will always want to play instead of work and then, when they lose the job, they'll be looking for a handout so they can play some more.

My dad taught me some interesting things. I don't think my dad had any want tos. I certainly don't think he ever allowed me to have any. All I remember is need tos. Everything about my life was what we needed to do.

My dad worked hard his whole life and I got a wonderful work ethic from him. He worked hard and ended up with nothing. What I learned out of that was not from the negative side, but I learned that working hard isn't everything. You also have to work smart. But I definitely learned that you have to do what you need to first, not what you want to. There does need to be time for your want tos. Stop and smell the roses. But you have to do the need tos first.

I grew up poor. We had a wood furnace in the basement and so, of course, we burned wood. That's what heated the house in the wintertime. Every Saturday morning, I had to go out to the wood pile and throw the wood in a wheelbarrow, haul it over to the basement window, throw it into the basement and stack it up so that we had wood for the rest of the week. If the woodpile was low, I had to go out into the woods and cut more.

I decided one day that I wanted to have a Saturday off. I knew what Dad had planned for Saturday, so I decided to get ahead of him. Monday night, I shoveled the walk all the way out to the wood pile and I split wood and loaded up the wheelbarrow. I hauled it over, dumped it in the basement and stacked it up. I did that every night all week. By the time I went to bed Friday night, the basement was full of wood. I was so excited because I would have a Saturday off.

Saturday morning came. At 5:30 in the morning, my dad woke me up. He said, "Son, thanks. You did a great job. The basement looks plum full. We got that done. You know, Mr. Brown, he's got arthritis real bad. He's up in his eighties. He can't get wood into his house. You know what? We need to go down there, cut some wood for him and fill his house."

We went down there from 5:30 in the morning until 9:00 that night. I said, "I ain't doing that no more." My dad found something to do every waking hour of my life. But through it all, I learned to do what I need to do before I do what I want to do.

> **If we could turn our affections on what we're doing and really love what we're doing, it becomes easy to be successful.**

Change Your Want Tos into Need Tos

We know that we need to do certain things before we do what we want to. That is a key to success. But when this becomes powerful, and easy, is when we turn our need tos into want tos. If we can turn our affections on what we're doing and really love what we're doing, it becomes easy to be successful. The truth is that I actually love to do what I need to. I recently had an opportunity to go skiing, but I passed it up because there was something else that I needed to do. But, quite honestly, I love what I needed to do, so it really wasn't a big deal. I love what I do.

How does that come to pass? How do you get to a place where you just love what you're doing? I believe that it all starts with something called the will of God.

In Matthew 26, we find Jesus in the Garden of Gethsemane. He said to His disciples, "Would you pray for an hour? I'm going to go over here and pray, too."

You can choose the will of God, which is the Word of God, and let it develop a desire.

The disciples did what they wanted to do, not what they needed to do. They all fell asleep.

Jesus went a little way from them and began to pray. When you read that whole passage, it is clear that Jesus did not want to go to the cross. His flesh did not want to have anything to do with the suffering and death. He earnestly asked God if there was any other way.

But there was a desire in Jesus that developed a passion. That passion motivated Him to His destiny and it made Him run His race. His passion made Him desire the will of God above all else.

I believe that we can all do the same thing. You can choose the will of God, which is the Word of God, and let it develop a desire. Jesus did what He needed to do, not what He wanted to do. His flesh so desired not to do it, that He sweated great drops of blood. But Jesus said, "Not my will, but Your will be done." When He submitted His will, it created a desire that produced a passion in Him and that passion produced the action to do the will of God.

How can you love what you do? First of all, begin to speak it. Submit your will to God's will to be excellent at your job, to be the best at whatever it is that you do. When I worked in sheet metal, I was the best sheet metal man I could be. When I worked in plumbing, I was the best plumber I could possibly be.

He wants you to become successful so that you can be blessed to be a blessing.

When I was a teacher, I was the best teacher that I could possibly be. I always developed a desire and a passion that motivated me to accomplish and to reach my destiny.

It doesn't matter what you are doing. You might hate your job. You might hate your boss. Well, change your thinking. Develop a desire for the will of God. Tell yourself, "God's got me here for a reason. He has me here for a purpose. It's part of my path and I'm going to run my race and develop a desire to be the best that I can."

You can get the same kind of desire for the Word of God. The first time I started reading the Word, I said it was the best cure for insomnia that I had ever found. It put me right to sleep. But the more I read and the more I understood it, the greater that I wanted to accomplish it. If you press into it, you will develop a desire for it. Today, there is not anything I have a greater passion for than the study of the Word. It's what I do on vacation. There is a passion for it that burns in me because I know that it is taking me to my destiny.

God wants you to have a fire and a passion that will take you to your destiny. He wants you to become success-ful so that you can be blessed to be a blessing. You begin by doing what you need to do before you do what you want to do. Then it becomes a passion that you want to do. It becomes a fire that burns inside of you.

The wealthy have a vision set on fire by passion. Get a vision. Get an idea. Believe God to run your race and reach your destiny. Continue to drive for excellence and, if you will do your need tos, they will become your want tos. If they line up with the will of God, success will never pass you by.

CHAPTER 11:

Seizing the Opportunity

We all have opportunities every day for increasing our wealth. The problem is that most of the time, we don't even recognize them as opportunities. Sometimes they are just interruptions in our day. When we do see them, most of the time, we just aren't ready to capitalize on them.

Some time ago, the Lord gave me a statement that I want to pass on to you.

Wealth is an appropriate reaction to an opportunity.

Another way of saying it might be something like this.

What is in us is the controlling factor of what is around us.

By that I mean that what is in us will determine how we react to an opportunity. If poverty is in us, we will respond inappropriately to that opportunity and it will be missed. But if prosperity is in us, then it will rise up and we'll react to the opportunity by taking advantage of it without much thought or question.

If you're not happy with what's around you, then maybe you need to change what's in you. Most of the time we just complain about our circumstances, but what is in us is the controlling factor that creates our circumstances. I like to equate it to your spouse. You are married to him or her rather than somebody else because of what is in you. The flaws in your mate are the reason that he or she couldn't do any better than you.

If you're not happy with what's around you, then maybe you need to change what's in you.

What is in us is producing what's around us. If we want to change what's around us, we're going to have to change some things that are in us.

I believe with my whole heart that we could see a dramatic difference in our lives if we just changed one thing. If we would do one productive thing every day for 365 days, in one year, our lives would be revolutionized. If we became productive in one thing in our families, one thing in our marriages, one thing with our children, one thing with our finances, one thing with our church, one thing with the Word, that's all it would take. You would be amazed at how life would change by the application of just one thing.

God's perfect plan for us is to start small and finish big. We all started as babies and finished bigger—some bigger than others. The Bible tells us to despise not small beginnings. We should get excited about starting where we're at and moving on to what God has for us. He said to be content in the situation that we're in, but that doesn't mean to be satisfied. We do need to start someplace.

Most people want to start big. I've met many pastors who want to start a church, but they don't want a small church with ten people. They want to start with 6,000. The problem is that they

Fast money can destroy people.

couldn't handle 6,000 because they never learned how to handle ten.

You have to be able to start your business at a small level and learn the multitude of things that are necessary for the business to be successful before you try to handle something bigger. You have to grow into it.

Get rich quick schemes make schemers rich at the expense of your greed. Fast money can destroy people. Quick wealth is dangerous to you, to your family and to your life.

But if you're willing to start somewhere and learn in the process, you can have a lot because you learn to handle the small amounts first. He who is faithful in a little will be made ruler over a lot.

One of the things you gain by starting small is experience. Experience isn't always pleasant, but it prepares you to handle problems. There's a reason why they associate gray hair with wisdom. Those with gray hair have experienced life.

Elvis used to sing, "Some kids born well are rich as

a king but I was born without a doggone thing but hard knocks." There's something to be said for hard knocks. You learn from them. If you learn at that level, you'll be able to control yourself and handle things at a higher level. It is a growth process.

To understand experience, consider a small child. You say to the child, "Don't touch the stove because it is hot and it will burn you." Now, children being children, as soon as you say, "Don't," they want to. But a small child may not know what hot means or what a burn is. Somewhere along the line, however that child will touch something hot and then he will know. And the burn will remind him for several days at least. He then has experience. Based on that experience, he won't touch the hot stove again.

We learn from experience. So experience is something that we should be happy about. That is why James says to call it all joy when you fall into various trials. Joy is the strength to overcome whatever the situation is and be happy about it because you know you're going to learn from it. It will prepare you for something better a little bit further down the line.

> **If you can't be thankful when you have virtually nothing, then you will not be thankful when you have something.**

By starting small, we learn thankfulness. If you can't be thankful when you have virtually nothing, then you will not be thankful when you have something. If the only thing you have is your health, you can still be thankful for that.

God desires that we be thankful all along the way. There is power in it.

When we start small, we learn something called discipline. We learn self-control. If you can discipline yourself to live on $200 a week and keep your bills current, good credit and food on the table, then you will be able to do just fine when you have $10,000 a week. But if you don't learn this at $200, you'll be in an even bigger mess with $10,000. You'll have lousy credit and you'll end up losing everything you've gained.

Starting small, you gain exposure. Exposure's an interesting word. You're exposed to so much more of life when you start with nothing and you work your way up to something. There's an exposure along the way that is teaching you things and training you.

Sometimes it is a matter of being exposed to things that will motivate you to never go back. When I was young, we lived in a line shack with no electricity, no running water and no indoor facilities. We had to stack hay bales against the side of the house so that we could keep the snow out and keep the house a little warmer. What may not be obvious from that description is that we were the richest in the community. We had food to eat. My dad made sure that we always had three meals a day, which was more than many in the area.

I used to deliver the local newspaper to make extra money. I made $3 a week. But I had to go into some of those houses, if you could call them that, to collect money for the paper. Often they would be cooking cabbage soup.

Those who were doing well could add a potato to it. Cabbage and potatoes were something that you could raise all summer and they would keep through the winter, so that was what many people lived on. The smell of boiling cabbage is one of the strongest memories of my childhood.

The exposure to that smell created a memory that stuck with me my whole life. I remember one day after we were married, Maureen decided to surprise me with cabbage soup. She did it because she loved me and thought it would be a pleasant surprise. She had no idea what that smell stirred up in me. I walked into the house, took one sniff and said, "I'll be back as soon as that smell and that soup are out of the house." That exposure was something that made me never want to go back to that kind of a life or anything that reminded me of it.

Another thing we learn is maturity. We grow mature. Slowly, as we begin to mature from small to great, we find out that life is not about us. It's about others.

By starting small, we learn to utilize our time effectively. Was the last minute that passed productive or was it wasted? That is the kind of question that God has asked me over the years so that I would constantly and consistently be productive with my time and not waste it. Every second that passes by is gone forever. It can't be made up. You can't go back and get it.

Starting small develops reliance on God. That is something that you absolutely need. And your dependence on God needs to continue your entire life. When you have a lot of money, you don't want to start depending on it instead of God. This is a natural tendency. That is why Jesus said that it is easier for a camel to go through the eye of a needle than for a rich man to enter the Kingdom of Heaven. He was warning us not to stop depending on God, no matter how much money we gain.

There are many reasons why starting small is good for you. Once things begin to multiply, you will be ready to handle it. God's plan for us is that

Starting small develops reliance on God.

He wants us to be fruitful and multiply and fill the earth. We work at a job to gain a seed that we can invest. As we invest, the money starts to multiply until it is working for us rather than us working for the money. The soil toils for us rather than us toiling for the soil.

The object is to begin multiplying. God is not into addition. He is into multiplication. There is a simple mathematical calculation that illustrates just how powerful multiplication can be.

If I were to work for you for thirty days, just for one month, starting with a daily wage of just one penny and doubling it every day, you might think that you were getting a good deal. And for the first few days, you would. At the end of the first day, you would owe me $.01. At the end of the second day, my wages would be another $.02. At the end of the third day, you would owe me another $.04. I would be making $.08 on the fourth day and $.16 on the fifth day. Adding up the daily totals for the first week, you would have paid me $1.27. At the end of two weeks, you would still have only paid me $163.83 total.

But after that, things would start to change. Just one week later, you would owe me $10,485.76 for the day. Added to the previous twenty days, that would be a total of $20,971.51. On the thirtieth day, you would have paid me a total for the month of $10,737,418.23. Multiplication works a lot faster than addition.

Programming the Subconscious

We talked earlier about the Parable of the Talent. You will recall that a man gave his servants each different amounts of money. The first got five talents, which he doubled to ten. The second was given two talents which he doubled to four. The third got one talent, with which he did nothing. He then had to defend himself and explain why he hadn't multiplied his money.

> *I was afraid, and went and hid your talent in the ground* (Matthew 25:25).

What was in him that would not allow him to change and take advantage of the opportunity? What comes up in you in similar situations that keeps you from taking advantage of opportunities?

I want to look again at a verse that you are very familiar with.

> *For as he thinks in his heart, so is he* (Proverbs 23:7).

The word "think" means a gatekeeper or a custodian

at the door. All of your senses feed information to your mind—everything that you are feeling, seeing, hearing, tasting, touching. Your mind then formulates thoughts based on that information.

The idea of thinking, being a gatekeeper, means that you have the ability to close the gate to certain things that come along and say, "No, I'm not going to think about that." That information then has to go away. Or you can open the gate and say, "Yes, I believe that. I receive it."

You can do that with any thoughts that come along. You can do it with lust. You say, "Oh, I like that," and it plants the seeds of lust in your heart and as a result, when that seed grows, it will have power over you.

You can also do this with prosperity. If you open the gate to thoughts of prosperity and receive them according to the Word, it becomes a seed that is planted in your life and, as it grows, it begins to affect you.

The next word I want to look at is "heart." Here, it means the breath of life, the living soul. We are each made up of body, soul and spirit. The soul is made up of mind, will and emotion. But there is another division in the realm of the soul—the conscious and the unconscious.

The conscious is receiving the thoughts and the information that affect the feelings, the mind, the will, and the thoughts. The subconscious takes care of things like your heartbeat. You don't stop and say, "Beat, heart. Beat, heart." It just happens. It is already programmed to life. When a baby is born, the subconscious is already wired to change every cell in the body every seven years. It can rebuild the entire body. You don't have to think about it.

Your subconscious does it automatically. Your subconscious runs your breathing.

The subconscious can be programmed not to support life. There is a man I know who told me about his daughter. She was a straight "A" student, graduated from high school with honors and was doing great in college. But she became suicidal. He told me that she had gotten over that, but then she had a sleeping problem. Whenever she went to sleep, she would forget to breathe and then she would lurche awake and gasp for air. They just couldn't understand what was happening. The problem was that she had spent that time programming her subconscious to death, not life. Even though she wasn't suicidal anymore, her subconscious was still programmed that way.

Your subconscious is what produces reactions. If someone throws something at you, you automatically react. You don't have to consciously think about it. You either catch it or dodge it.

I was golfing with my son, Jason, one day when he was about twelve years old. I was standing by the pin next to the hole, because I figured that it was the safest place on the course. Jason was in a sand trap. He hit the ball and all I saw was the ball right in front of me. I caught it. There wasn't time to think about it. I just caught it. It hurt, but I caught it. It was faster than thought.

You drive down the road and suddenly a car pulls out in front of you. You whip the wheel around, step on the gas, nail the brakes, whip around the other car and continue on. How did that happen? You didn't have time to think about it. It was a reaction produced in the subconscious.

You can program anything into your subconscious. In the service, I was trained for self-defense and I spent a number of years studying Tai Kwon Do. Later, in college, I was in an art class with a very good friend. He was a gentle-natured, nice guy. We were headed down to a basement where a lab was set up for glass-blowing. He had gone ahead of me. It was dark in the area of the basement. As I came down the hallway, he jumped out and said, "Boo!"

Before I could think about what I was doing, I kicked him in the stomach. I repented of it, but it was a conditioned response to the circumstance. It was faster than my thoughts. There are people who can catch an arrow. It is the subconscious that is programmed to react.

> **The subconscious can command the body to do supernatural things.**

The subconscious can command the body to do supernatural things. There are true stories of incredible feats. A woman was in a car wreck and her little boy was pinned under a two-ton car. Faster than she could think about it, she picked up the car and rolled it off of her son. If she had consciously thought about it, she never could have done it. It was something that was programmed into her subconscious.

There was a commuter plane flying into San Francisco. It had a full load of people. As they came in for a landing, about 2,000 feet off the runway, they lost an engine. It is a dangerous situation anywhere, but that close to the ground, it is especially bad. The force of the other engine causes the plane to yaw. The two engines balance each other out, but when one stops, it is likely to flip the plane over into the ground.

The copilot froze and did nothing. The pilot took over and did a number of things in just a matter of seconds that enabled him to get control of the plane and bring it down safely.

When interviewed later, the copilot said that he froze. He just didn't know what to do. There was no time to correct it. That was what was in him and it produced his reaction—nothing. He remembered watching the pilot. All he could see was a blur. He couldn't even see his hands move, they were so fast.

When they asked the pilot how he managed to do all that in just a few seconds, he replied that he didn't know. He said that it seemed like he had plenty of time. He did a complete systems check, everything that he was trained to do, and then landed the plane. That was what was in him. That is what his training had programmed his subconscious to do.

Now, I want you to take this concept and apply it to your life. If you program your subconscious with wealth, then it will react to opportunities with wealth. It will take advantage of them. When prosperity and wealth are foremost in you and an opportunity sails by, your immediate reaction will be to produce wealth from the opportunity.

If you change what's in you, then it will change what's around you. Your brain needs washing. You need to reprogram it. You need to fill it with the Word. It's not enough just to think about the Word. You need to have it programmed into your subconscious. When your subconscious is programmed right, your automatic reaction to life will always be to overcome.

Wealth is an appropriate reaction to an opportunity. Program yourself to react that way.

CHAPTER 12:

The Mind and the Heart

We are made up of body, soul and spirit. Our problems really occur in the soul. The body is just dirt. Your spirit is born again. It has everything it needs. It doesn't need love. It doesn't need validation. It is in complete communication with God. The problems are in the soul. It is made up of mind, will and emotion. That's where we find the thoughts, the feelings and the decision making process.

It is so critical to life that we understand the part the subconscious plays that we need to examine it in great depth. It can affect every part of your existence. You go to the doctor and he tells you that you have cancer. What is your immediate reaction? What is programmed into your subconscious?

If you have programmed yourself with the Word of God, the immediate reaction is, "By His stripes I'm healed. I can't have cancer." The reaction surfaces before you have time to think about it. Your conscious mind might have thoughts about it, but your subconscious controls your immediate reaction.

The problem is that it takes an ounce of information to form a perception and a ton to change it. Once you have programmed something into your subconscious, it will require some effort to change it. But if it is wrong, then you need to change.

Too many of us have grown up with some wrong patterns programmed in. They were patterns that you learned as a child. Some can be very destructive. Your dad had a heart attack. Your grandfather had a heart attack. You think that you will probably have a heart attack. And you probably will if you don't change that programming with the Word of God.

Use your conscious mind to plant the right seeds in your subconscious.

If you grew up believing that God wanted you to be sick, then you will not have an appropriate response when you find out that you are sick. If you grew up believing that God wants you to be poor, you will not have an appropriate response to an opportunity for wealth. You will stay poor.

Just learning a verse of the Bible in your conscious mind will not produce the reaction. You don't capture faith in your mind. It must be written on your heart. Your thoughts and feelings are constantly changing, but your subconscious reactions change very slowly. When your subconscious is programmed right, that is a good thing. When it is not, you need to begin changing it. You need to reprogram it by constantly quoting the Word, dwelling on it, meditating on it. Get it into your heart. Use your conscious mind to plant the right seeds in your subconscious. The conscious is a seed planter. The subconscious is the garden.

I've spoken at some length about this, but we need to see it in the Word. In fact, it is a principle that permeates all of Scripture. At one point in His ministry, Jesus was confronted by some people who asked Him some questions. One of the questions was, "Which is the great commandment in the law?" (Matthew 22:36). In other words, what are the principles of God that we're supposed to live by?

The Old Testament has Ten Commandments. Jesus grouped them together into two categories, to keep it simple.

> *Jesus said to him, "You shall love the LORD your God with all your heart, with all your soul, and with all your mind." This is the first and great commandment. And the second is like it: "You shall love your neighbor as yourself." On these two commandments hang all the Law and the Prophets* (Matthew 22:37).

We are spirit. We know that everything in the spirit already loves God. So the only thing that Jesus could be talking about concerning the heart is the soul. The soul has mind, will and emotions and the will has a conscious and a subconscious.

Jesus mentions two specific things—the mind and the heart. These correspond to the conscious and the subconscious. Everything issues out of the heart, not the mind. You change your mind and you can't change anything. You change your heart and you can change everything.

So the mind can be changed. Thoughts are changed easily. Reactions, however, are changed rather slowly. When you raise children, you want to form the right reaction in their subconscious so that when they're confronted with a crisis in life, they will respond faster than a thought, faster than a feeling. Then they will respond appropriately to the circumstance or the situation.

We program many things into our children. How they grow up thinking about money is the result of what we program into them. The work ethic that they develop is based on what we program into them. Either we're programming a reaction of right work ethics, working hard, starting early and quitting late, or we're programming a reaction of grumbling and complaining about their boss and their miserable work. Which it is will depend on which they see us doing. If your attitude is, "I can't wait till the weekend gets here and we can get away and play," then don't be surprised if your child, when he hits sixteen or seventeen years old, wants to play instead of work. It's what you programmed into his subconscious. That will be your children's reaction to life.

It is the same with morality. What are you programming by your life and example? When your daughter is somewhere in a parked car and the opportunity is there, you want something in her subconscious to rise up and say, "No. I'm not doing that until I'm married." But if there is immorality in the home, then you are programming the wrong thing and you will probably get the wrong result.

You want to program the right reaction into your child before the opportunity comes along.

It's never too late to begin changing the programming that is in you, but you do need to start planting the right seeds there now. Do it in yourself and in your children. The mind can be changed easily. Behavior issues come from the heart.

Written on the Heart

We see this combination of the heart and the mind in the Old Testament as well.

> *I, the LORD, search the heart,*
> *I test the mind.*
> *Even to give every man according to his ways,*
> *According to the fruit of his doings.*
> (Jeremiah 17:10)

"Search" means to penetrate, to examine intimately the heart. The heart, in the Hebrew, means the innermost part. That's why the Bible says to go to your closet and close the door to pray. You are to search your innermost heart and find out what you believe because that is the only thing you'll be able to receive. You won't receive out of your head. You receive from the heart, the subconscious.

But it also says that God tests the mind. The word "mind" means the steering part. The mind is the controlling part. It is the seed planter to the subconscious. It is where you determine what will go into the subconscious to program it. It is literally the steering part of what's prepared. In other words, your mind and your thoughts determine what will be planted in your heart.

The next line has the word "give." The word here means to allow. He says, "Even to give," or "to allow every man according to his ways."

The word "ways" means the choice or the course of life. God allows you to live the life you choose. It is "according to the fruit of his doings." God won't cross your will. He won't make you prosperous until it's a part of your innermost heart.

The heart is mentioned again in Proverbs.

Let not mercy and truth forsake you;
Bind them around your neck,
Write them on the tablet of your heart.
(Proverbs 3:3)

The tablet here refers to a polished, smooth surface, possibly stone or wood. In order to write on it, you would have to scratch or carve. So He says, "Write My precepts, write mercy and write the truth of the Word on this hard polished surface." Have you ever carved your initials into a desktop? It takes a lot of work to get it out. You have to sand and grind. It doesn't come out easily. God says to engrave His precepts on your heart so that they can't be gotten out easily.

God is anxious for us to get His truth out of our minds and into our hearts. That is what He says He wants for us.

> *This is the covenant that I will make with them after those days, says the LORD: I will put My laws into their hearts, and in their minds I will write them* (Hebrews 10:16).

God says that He will write His laws in the seed planting process of the conscious mind as well as in the subconscious, if we'll allow it. How does faith come? It comes by hearing and hearing. It has to undo all the fear and the doubt and unbelief that are already written on your heart. All of that has to be ground off and replaced with the truth of the Word.

God says to engrave His precepts on your heart so that they can't be gotten out easily.

For many years, Maureen and I have played tapes of Scripture continuously in our home. We play it while we are sleeping. We play it all the time. The reason is that we are constantly reprogramming our subconscious with the Word.

You can check your subconscious by remembering your dreams. Your conscious mind goes to sleep, but your subconscious keeps producing all night and it will bring to the surface whatever is there and reveal to you the intentions of your heart. If you have fear, you will have fearful dreams. If you have peace, you will have peaceful dreams.

I have had the Word in my sleep for so long now that I often wake up laughing out loud. The joy is a part of my heart, not just my mind.

We see this pairing of the mind and the heart again in Hebrews 4:12, a verse that is very familiar to most Christians.

> *For the word of God is living and powerful, and sharper than any two-edged sword, piercing even to the division of soul and spirit, and of joints and marrow, and is a discerner of the thoughts and intents of the heart* (Hebrews 4:12).

Again, it's not just the thoughts, the seed planter, but it is also the garden of the subconscious where the intention lies. You may have been struggling with something like smoking, for example. Your thoughts are that you have been intending to quit, but the flesh is still struggling. In the intentions of the heart, however, you plant the seed that God calls your body His temple and anything harmful you do to it is wrong. Now that intention grows in the heart and in due time, it will cause the reaction of quitting smoking. The Word will sand out the junk.

The thoughts of the mind are the conscious. The heart is the subconscious.

> *My son, give attention to my words;*
> *Incline your ear to my sayings.*
> *Do not let them depart from your eyes;*
> *Keep them in the midst of your heart;*

For they are life to those who find them,
And health to all their flesh.
Keep your heart with all diligence.
For out of it spring the issues of life.
Put away from you a deceitful mouth,
And put perverse lips far from you.
(Proverbs 4:20-24)

Here again, God tells us to keep our hearts right. Keep the programming in your subconscious positive. Keep it filled with the Word. How do we do that? Get rid of a deceitful mouth and perverse lips. Your mouth, your tongue, your thoughts, your vision, your words, have the power of death and life. They are what determine the seed that will be planted in your subconscious.

It is from your heart that the issues of life spring. It is extremely important that you keep life written there. It is the heart that produces faith.

For assuredly, I say to you, whoever says to this mountain, "Be removed and be cast into the sea," and does not doubt in his heart, but believes that those things he says will be done, he will have whatever he says (Mark 11:23).

It says whoever "does not doubt in his heart." It is the reaction that is faster than a thought. You may have some doubts in your mind and your feelings may change from day to day or after somebody's laid hands on you. You felt the presence of God, but as soon as you left church, you had all kinds of other thoughts. But if it is written on your heart, if you believe it in your heart, you will continue to react.

Last Line of Defense

I hope that you are beginning to see that this is not just some isolated verse somewhere in the Bible. It is a principle that runs through every part of Scripture. Let me close these thoughts with one more picture of how it all works.

God placed Adam and Eve in the Garden of Eden. Eden was a place and the Garden was a place in Eden, much like your soul is a place, but there's a garden in your soul. In the Garden, God placed the tree of life and the tree of the knowledge of good and evil and gave Adam and Eve a choice between them. It is a choice that you make every day.

What protects this Garden is the power of the will. The will is your last line of defense for the seed that you've prepared to plant in your garden. The will can determine whether or not to allow that seed in.

Adam and Eve chose the tree of the knowledge of good and evil as opposed to the tree of life. When we look at the New Testament, we see the conscious mind with the will and emotions, and the subconscious where we plant the seeds of life—health, joy, peace, and prosperity. This is the soulish realm. It is Eden in the New Testament. This is your Garden of Eden.

The seed is the Word. The thoughts and the vision that you have are what become the seed. What you plant as seed is what you will do in deed. If you want success, if you want too much, you have to start paying attention to what you are planting in the garden of your heart. Plant prosperity and you will reap prosperity.

CHAPTER 13:

Uploading Your Download

A number of years ago, I went skiing with my son, Scot, and Dave, a friend of his. Dave had never been skiing before, but we just strapped some skis on him and took him up to one of the highest mountains. He was sitting between us and as we got to the top, he got off the lift and fell down pretty quickly. That wasn't much of a surprise, since he had not trained for it at all.

In order to miss him, I had to ski off to the side and I landed on a pylon and broke four ribs loose from my sternum. They rolled in and pressed against my heart and put pressure on it and started to cause water and fluid to build up.

I love skiing, though, so I decided to keep going. In fact, I skied all day. Once I got out on the slopes, my chest loosened up a little and felt better, but the pain got pretty bad when I got on a lift again. But I stuck it out to the end of the day.

When we got back home, I went to the doctor. He examined me and said, "You traumatized your heart. You had a heart attack. The whole thing is a mess. You'll be lucky to end up in a wheel chair because the damage is so bad."

I called the elders of the church over and they prayed for me, according to Scripture. I got medicine that I was supposed to take that would regulate my heartbeat.

It was on New Year's Day that I woke up and I couldn't get my head off the pillow because I would pass out every time I tried. I took my pulse and it was down around thirty beats a minute. I got so dizzy that I couldn't stand.

My wife took me to the emergency room and the doctors ran all of their tests on my heart and couldn't find anything wrong. They said it was the medicine that was causing the problem. I was completely healed and have been ever since.

The reason I'm telling you this story, however, is not to talk about healing. There is an important aspect to this that I want you to grasp. They kept me in the hospital until the medicine wore off and then they sent me home.

I was physically fine, but for the next year and a half, my conscious mind did not trust my unconscious to run my heart. I could hear my heart beat twenty-four hours a day. I could hear the blood flow in my veins. I became painfully aware of it. I would try to sleep at night and all I could hear was my heart pumping. Every once in a while it would skip a beat and I would think, *Am I going to die?* I would jump up out of bed, thinking that if I moved, I could get my heart beat again. There was nothing wrong with it. It is normal for the heart to do that occasionally, but it played on my conscious thoughts. Fear would rise in me.

I had to work diligently with the Word for more than a year to build the wall back up between the conscious and the subconscious so that the conscious could once again trust the subconscious to operate. I had to reprogram my subconscious.

As a man thinks, feels and believes, so is his condition of mind, body and circumstance. In other words, your thoughts are affecting your mind. Your feelings are affecting your body and your belief system is producing the circumstance or the effects of what you planted in your heart.

If you can get the right things into your subconscious, then your conscious can trust it. Though fear might come into your feelings or doubt rise up in your thoughts, they do not control your reactions. The

> **As a man thinks, feels and believes, so is his condition of mind, body and circumstance.**

Word of God that has been engraved on your heart, your subconscious, takes precedence and you react accordingly. When there is an opportunity for wealth, your subconscious reacts faster than your thoughts and says, "Let's do it." This means that we have to program our hard drive. We want to build the right stuff in us.

Have you ever wondered why people are so different from one another? One person is happy and another is sad. One person is prosperous and another is poor. One is shy and another confident. One lives in luxury and another in great want. One is a failure and another is a great success. One stays sick and another gets healed. One has constant crisis after crisis and another seems to sail through life without any big problems.

People are always changing their conscious thoughts, hoping that by thinking positive, it will improve things. The problem is that thoughts keep changing. You might be a Republican today, a Democrat tomorrow, an Independent the next day, and wanting to move to France the next. Your thoughts are that fast and that unstable. You can be happily married today and ready to get a divorce tomorrow, just because some incident created an argument. The problem is in what has been programmed into your subconscious. If you would plant love in your heart, then it would rise up as the immediate reaction and it would overcome the negative thoughts. The battle is in our minds.

> *For it is the God who commanded light to shine out of darkness, who has shone in our hearts to give the light of the knowledge of the glory of God in the face of Jesus Christ. But we have this treasure in earthen vessels, that the excellence of the power may be of God and not of us* (2 Corinthians 4:6-7).

The earthen vessel is your body. It is the dirt that you are made of. It is our temporary dwelling of clay. We are body, soul and spirit. The body is going back to dust. The spirit has been reborn and is completely new. The soul is the part that is changing. The key is to program the subconscious with the Word so that it can relate directly to the spirit. The agreement of the two will produce the right reaction to the circumstance, whether it be negative or positive.

That is reprogramming the hard drive. It is the Word of God that does it. The Word is the "excellence of the power" that is in "earthen vessels." It is God who reprograms us, not we who do it for ourselves. God designed it that way so that you can never say, "Hey, look what I did!" It is the Word in us that does the work.

If someone shouts at you in anger, there is a reaction that comes up out of you. You don't even have time to think about it. It just comes out. It comes from what Jesus called "the abundance of the heart."

> *Brood of vipers! How can you, being evil, speak good things? For out of the abundance of the heart the mouth speaks. A good man out of the good treasure of his heart brings forth good things, and an evil man out of the evil treasure brings forth evil things* (Matthew 12:34-35).

Out of what you have programmed into your subconscious, the mouth speaks. It is a response that is faster than thought. If someone swings at you, you don't think about your response. You don't consciously think, "I will block that, then I will hit back." No, you instantly block and swing without thought. It is programmed into your subconscious. That response does what it needs to do. It's not connected to thought or to feeling. It is coming right out of the abundance of the heart.

Verse 35 said that a good man brings forth good things out of the abundance of his heart. Again, we see a reaction that is based on what has been planted in the subconscious. Whenever you have thoughts consistently, those thoughts turn into seed that is planted in the soil of the subconscious and those seeds produce after their kind. If you have unforgiveness, offense and judgment, and that's all that you ever have in your thoughts, then that will program your reaction to other people or circumstances. If you constantly develop thoughts of joy, love, peace and all the good things of God, then those are the seeds that are planted and that will determine your reaction.

We have to plant the right things in the treasure house if we want the right response to come out of us.

We have to plant the right things in the treasure house if we want the right response to come out of us. It is a simple rule of cause and effect. It works in the spiritual world the same way that it happens in the physical. If you plant the right stuff, that is the cause, and it will create an effect.

I understand that there may be times when someone else affects your life in an adverse way. Someone runs into your car, for example. That wasn't something that you had any control over. You didn't do it. That person caused you physical damage. But if the Word of God is planted in you, then you can alter the effect of what someone else did.

There is a story of a farmer who had a favorite mule. One day the mule fell into a dry well. He began braying and howling and crying out. The farmer was desperate. He tried everything he could think of to get his mule out of that well. He tried to lasso the mule but it didn't work. Nothing he tried had any success.

Darkness came and finally, the farmer resigned himself to the loss of the mule. He said, "Well, the least that I can do is give my old mule a decent burial." So all through the night, the farmer shoveled dirt into the hole to bury his mule.

But the mule, down in the bottom of the hole, felt the dirt on his back. Every time a shovel full hit him, he shook it off of his back and trampled it under his feet. By morning, the mule just walked out of the hole.

The moral of the story is that the cause was something out of the mule's control, but he altered the effect. This is what God wants us to do. Someone else may cause things to happen in your life, but you have the power within you to change the effect. How do you deal with the dirt that somebody sends your way? It will all depend on what you have programmed into your subconscious. If you have the Word of God programmed in, you will realize that those who sling mud are just losing ground.

The thing that we have to do is learn to control our thoughts so that we are constantly planting the right seed.

> *For though we walk in the flesh, we do not war according to the flesh. For the weapons of our warfare are not carnal but mighty in God for pulling down strongholds, casting down*

*arguments and every high thing that exalts itself
against the knowledge of God, bringing every
thought into captivity to the obedience of Christ*
(2 Corinthians 10:3-5).

Our weapons are not in the natural realm. They are
spiritual. That means the Word. That is our primary weap-
on, the only one that will be effective. It is the Word that
will pull down strongholds.

What are strongholds? Many times we think that it refers to a stronghold in our minds, but that's not it. Your
mind is not capable of doing too much. You can see that
every New Year's Day when you make resolutions. None
of them worked because you tried to do them with your
mind. You have decided a hundred times that you will quit
smoking, but you are still smoking. Or you quit smoking
and now you eat too much. You just traded one addiction
for another.

There is still something programmed in your heart that
needs to change. The stronghold is in your subconscious.
In order to change it, you have to reprogram it. This is true
for any kind of problem that you struggle with. If you have
a problem with anger, it is because anger is programmed
into your subconscious. You have to change the program.
If you have a problem with lust, it is because lust is programmed into your heart. You have to change the programming.

We want to get rid of those strongholds. How do we do
it? By bringing every thought into captivity to the anointed

one, Christ Jesus. Every time a wrong thought pops up, you say, "No, I'm not going to think that. I'm going to think according to the Word." As you begin to control your thoughts, you will change the seed that is planted in your heart and it will drive the strongholds out.

This is why Paul said that we should determine what our thoughts dwell on.

> *Finally, brethren, whatever things are true, whatever things are noble, whatever things are just, whatever things are pure, whatever things are lovely, whatever things are of good report, if there is any virtue and if there is anything praiseworthy—meditate on these things* (Philippians 4:8).

We are to think on those things because it will reprogram our hard drives and we will start to get different reactions to the circumstances of life.

Enrico Caruso was one of the greatest opera singers of all time. During the first twenty years of the twentieth century, he was one of the most popular singers in any genre. He made 260 recordings and made millions of dollars from the sale of 78 rpm records. He was considered one of the greatest artists of his era.

While he was training, however, his voice coach told him to forget about it. He would never be able to sing. Rather than give up singing, he changed coaches. But those seeds were trying to be planted in his heart.

When it came time for his first major concert, the first time that it was more than a small group listening, he sat in the back room shaking in fear. The thought of singing in front of 2,000 people terrified him. It was the result of those thoughts trying to come back.

Someone listening to him recorded that at some point, he stood up and said, "The little me is afraid that people are going to laugh and that I can't sing. But the big me is going to rise up and the big me can sing." The "big me" was his subconscious. It had been trained. It had been programmed. It could sing just fine. He went out with that attitude. What had been programmed in his heart through training overcame the negative thoughts of the vocal coach. He went on to be the greatest of his time.

No matter what your mind might be saying—your thoughts, your fears, your doubts—if you program the right reaction, then when the crisis comes, your subconscious will rise up and say, "The big God in me is bigger than any circumstance, bigger than any situation, all powerful, more than a conqueror."

Your subconscious mind works twenty-four hours a day to make provision for your benefit. It is constantly pouring fruit into your lap. The question is, what fruit is it pouring out? It will only be able to harvest what you have planted. If you don't like the fruit that you've got, you need to change the seed. You can't keep planting corn and expect peas. It won't happen. You've got to plant the right stuff.

CHAPTER 14:

The Power of Suggestion

I remember an incident that happened when I was about eight years old. I was out playing with my glove and a ball. I threw the ball in the air and caught it over and over.

My dad had just built two log cabins, hand hewn, notched together, from the ground up. They were next to our home and he planned to rent them out. He had made a metal sign trimmed with wood and he had painted it all white and was in the process of painting "For Rent, Day or Week" on it in bright red letters. He laid the sign down on the lawn where he could tape off the letters. He had the brush and the open can of paint sitting there next to him, right where I was throwing the ball in the air and catching it.

He said to me, "Son, don't throw the ball up here because you're going to miss the ball. It's going to bounce, hit the paint and the paint will spill all over the sign."

Being an eight-year-old boy, I knew that I would not miss the ball. And even if I did, the odds of that little ball bouncing exactly right to hit that can were astronomical.

So I didn't take his warning too seriously.

But wouldn't you know, the very next time I tossed the ball up, it hit the end of the glove, bounced once, hit the can and spilled bright red paint all over the sign. And of course, trauma followed.

From that incident, I understood something about the power of suggestion.

Webster's Dictionary gives the definition of "suggestion"—"Suggestion is the act or the instance of putting something into one's mind, the process of a thought, an idea, suggesting to entertain, accept and then put into effect."[1] In other words, when a suggestion is made, it can be entertained. It can be received as truth. It can be believed. Then it can become conceived, and then it will produce an action. That is how the process works. What you plant as seed is what you will do in deed.

The world has been utilizing the power of suggestion for hundreds and hundreds of years. All of advertisement is nothing more than the power of suggestion at work. The mere suggestion can make you want the product.

There have been laws passed to prohibit subliminal advertising. They used to pop the words "You're thirsty for a Coke" on the screen at drive-in theatres. It was there for a single frame every so often, so fast that your conscious mind couldn't detect it. But the subconscious could pick it up and before long, you had to go and get a Coke. It is all about the suggestion that you plant in your subconscious.

We have typically considered the Bible to be a book

---

1 Merriam-Webster's Dictionary, S.V. "Suggestion."

of commandments from God about how to live. But God is really concerned with getting the Word into our subconscious where it will affect our reactions. It is really a book of suggestions. You don't have to follow anything in it. You have a choice. You don't have to get saved. You can make whatever decision you want. But God gave us a book of suggestions to have life. We have to receive them before they have any effect.

"By His stripes we are healed" is a suggestion for you to have health and wholeness. But you have to receive it. It has to become entertained and accepted for it to be put into effect. It has to be written on your heart, not just in your mind. Then it will be a reaction, faster than a thought.

> **The only place that you should submit your will is to the Word of God.**

A hypnotist understands better than most of the body of Christ how suggestion works. A hypnotist will go to his audience and say, "Is there anyone "willing" to be hypnotized?" He uses the word willing because it is critical that the will be submitted to the action. As soon as the individual gets up to go, he has made some form of decision to submit his will. That is the most dangerous thing that a person can do. The only place that you should submit your will is to the Word of God. Jesus gave us the example in the Garden of Gethsemane when He said, "Not my will, but Your will be done." He submitted to the Word, not to anything else. You should not even submit your will to your mate. It is your last line of defense between your conscious and your subconscious.

As soon as the hypnotist gets people on stage, he says something like, "Now, just sit down. Get comfortable and concentrate." Then he starts to swing something in front of them, some object. What is the point of that? It is to get the conscious mind to focus on something so that you empty your head enough to have no negative thought contrary to what he's trying to do. He gets you visually focused on the repetition of the object swinging back and forth and he says, "You're getting sleepy." Before long, you're asleep.

At that point, he's entered the subconscious mind. That person is in a hypnotic state. He can make a suggestion to the subconscious and it is planted directly without any interference from the will. The will has been put to sleep. He can say, "You're a dog," and the person will start barking. The power of that suggestion is now working in the subconscious.

There are some limitations to what he can do, however. Because the subconscious is where the belief system lives, he can never get you to do anything contrary to your moral values or your belief system. But he can plant seeds there that can start to grow over time. It is the power of suggestion.

This is the danger in various forms of fortune telling. Most Christians know that they shouldn't dabble with horoscopes or ouija boards or astrology, but few understand why. The moment you pick up the newspaper and look at your horoscope, you've put a suggestion in your mind. If it says, "Don't leave the house today or you'll have an accident," it puts a fear in you. You stay home all day until you have to pick the kids up from school. Then you drive so carefully that you end up being too cautious and have an accident. When you open yourself up to these forms of fortune telling, you connect to the power of suggestion and if you receive it, you could potentially conceive it and act on it. It is only a small step further to the problem with false prophets. I believe in prophecy. Prophets are a part of the five-fold ministry of the church. There are prophets who are valid.

But there are also false prophets. There are people who delight in giving personal prophecies to others. They can be a good thing if they are uplifting and encouraging and centered in the Word. But there are many in the church who do not prophecy the Word of God. They will say things like, "God showed me that you are to sell all that you have, take your family, and move to Greenland to start a church."

Your first reaction should be, "Why didn't God tell me that personally?" You should never subject yourself to another person's will for your life. In fact, I am even careful about who I allow to pray for me. I don't want to submit myself to the power of suggestion from other people.

The reason that false prophets are sometimes successful is because we want to please God. When we get a personal prophecy, we start to think that if it is from God, we want to listen. That's when we get into trouble. You have not only the right to question and judge the prophecy, you have a responsibility to discern. If it doesn't line up with the Word and with what you already know God is doing in your life, then don't even listen.

There was a man who took his family on a vacation trip

to India. They saw the sights, visited the Taj Mahal and had a great time. At one point, his family dared him to get his fortune told by a local mystic. He eventually decided it might be fun, so he paid the fee and sat down. The lady began to read his lifeline. She was shocked and said, "Oh, my. Short." She looked up at him and said, "You're going to have a heart attack before the next new moon."

They all laughed about it and how silly an idea it was. But they decided to cut the vacation a little short and headed back to the United States. Once there, the man kept thinking about the fortune. He thought it would be a good idea to get all of his affairs in order, not because he believed the fortune teller, but just in case. He went to the doctor and had a complete check up to see if his heart was okay. The doctor said that everything was fine. There was nothing wrong with his heart at all.

> **You have to be careful what you allow into your subconscious because you could potentially believe it.**

But before the new moon, he died of a heart attack.

It was not that the fortune teller could predict the future. It was rather that the power of suggestion could create the future. You have to be careful what you allow into your subconscious because you could potentially believe it. And if you believe it, it will produce an effect in your life that you might not want.

Doers of the Word

James talks about the power of suggestion and how it works in temptation. In the first chapter, he makes the statement that God does not tempt people. Then he explains just how people are tempted.

> *But each one is tempted when he is drawn away by his own desires and enticed. Then, when desire has conceived, it gives birth to sin; and sin, when it is full-grown, brings forth death* (James 1:14-15).

Let's look at a couple of words from those verses. The first is the word "tempted." Temptation is nothing more than a whispered suggestion. The enemy comes along and says, "You see that guy's wife?" He comes to a girl and says, "See that woman's husband?" Something connects. It connects because the temptation is received and believed. The enticement begins to generate itself into a received condition that conceives. Then somewhere down the road, the enemy brings the opportunity for what was received to be acted on. By then, it is in the heart, in the subconscious, part of the programming, and the response to the opportunity is inappropriate.

This is what Jesus meant when he said that anyone who looks at a woman with lust has already committed adultery in his heart (Matthew 5:28). It is already in the subconscious and as soon as the opportunity presents itself, the response will be adultery.

It is not a matter of what is in your conscious mind. James goes on to say that your heart has to be involved.

But be doers of the word, and not hearers only, deceiving yourselves. For if anyone is a hearer of the word and not a doer, he is like a man observing his natural face in a mirror; for he observes himself, goes away, and immediately forgets what kind of man he was (James 1:22-24).

We have to "do" the word, a response of the heart, not just "hear" it, the action of the conscious mind. James describes a man seeing his natural face in a mirror. He walks away and forgets what kind of man he "was," past tense. If the thought is only retained in the mind and it is never planted in the subconscious, is never believed and received, it will never produce an appropriate reaction. Hearers only hear but the natural mind, the conscious mind, forgets. The subconscious does not.

You might ask, then, what about the Scripture that says we are supposed to forget those things that are behind and press on to those things that are ahead (Philippians 3:13)? The word "forget" in that verse means to transpose. In other words, it means to cover up. You may have physical abuse, sexual abuse, or some other terrible things in your past. The Word of God transposes those, covers them up and eliminates them from your subconscious. He replaces them with the Word so that you no longer react from the past. You react from the Word.

That is the only way that Paul could have said, "I have

no blood on my hands." He had killed a lot of people before he got into the Kingdom of God, but he still could say that he was right before God. He had transposed what Jesus did over the top of what was there in his heart.

You can overcome whatever circumstances have been buried in you. Just get enough of the Word to transpose your future over the top of your past and get on with your life.

The Lord has given you the power to obtain wealth—not just a little wealth, but too much wealth. When thoughts are received and the will is submitted, it passes the thoughts and the feelings as believed, as truth, and it agrees with your spirit. What you have received is what you will begin to act out and begin to do. That is how faith operates.

The Word suggests something to you. It suggests wealth, health, joy, peace, life and love. If you will receive that, it will change your subconscious and cause a completely different response to every situation in life. If you don't have the right response, then get the Word of God into you and change what is in your heart

CONCLUSION:

A World of Too Much

It is God's plan for His people to be prosperous. It is important that we understand why God wants us to be prosperous. He wants us to be blessed so that we can be a blessing. He wants us to have too much so that we have the ability to be generous on every occasion.

It is unfortunate that so many are convinced that God wants them to be poor and sick. They justify their poverty by pointing to greed as a horrible sin and claiming that they would rather do the will of God than be rich. I hope you have understood by now that it is impossible to do the will of God without resources. That is the reason God wants us to have them. It is for the sake of the house of the Lord that we seek prosperity (Psalm 122:9). God said very clearly that if we will seek His Kingdom first, then He will add all of the other things to us. Our motivation has to be for the sake of the Kingdom or wealth will control us, not the other way around.

We live in a land of great opportunity. It is a nation based on a system called capitalism, which, by definition, is characterized by private ownership, private decision, private investment and competition in a free market. That means that if you are not prosperous, it is not God's fault and it is not the government's fault. The opportunity is there. The problem is that you have not chosen to avail yourself of it.

There are many reasons why so many people fail to choose wealth. A significant problem is that we have all gone through an education system that has not really educated us. We have become intellectual. We have learned facts and information, but we haven't learned what to do with it. We haven't learned how to think.

The gaining of knowledge is an important first step but we then need to move on to understanding, which is gaining a grasp of why and how things work. We need to learn how business operates and how money works. We need to learn the world system.

Then, we need to add wisdom to our knowledge and our understanding. Knowledge means that we learn information so that we know something. Understanding means that we understand what we know. Wisdom means that we do what we understand that we know. We have to act or we will never achieve success.

We, like Abraham, have to make a choice. We have to choose between being blessed or being cursed. We have to get out or walk away from the wilderness of our past and leave behind the family pedigree or heritage that has kept us in poverty. We have to move on to the promises of God. It is a choice that we must make. Abraham was expected to be a blessing to all nations. We are, too.

Jesus sent us into the world to accomplish the same thing—to bless others. He said that He sent us as sheep among wolves, but we have seen that what He meant by that was that He wants us to be the first, to rise to the top. He wants us to be wise in learning how the world system works so that we can take advantage of it and bring the wealth into the Kingdom to accomplish His work.

We saw this pattern in the life of Joseph. He had every reason to sit down and quit. His brothers hated him. They sold him into slavery. He was falsely accused and ended up in prison. Yet he had a vision from God and he never lost sight of it. He excelled in everything that he did and ended up in charge of all of Egypt. One person committed to a dream is all that God needs to change the world. You have to have a dream, a vision of success.

Once Joseph was in power, he prepared for the future by accumulating great stores of grain and food. He bought low and, when famine came, he sold high. This is the most basic of all business principles. Joseph used common sense and by the time he was finished, he had all the money of Egypt, all the livestock and all the land.

The greatest enemy that any of us faces is comfort. We get comfortable in having enough and that keeps us from ever having a real vision of where God would like to take us. Even when we do have a dream, we never get around to pursuing it.

Never get comfortable with where you are. It will keep you from being motivated into the promises of God. It will keep you from ever having too much.

The biggest reason that we seek comfort is fear. We are simply afraid of losing what we have. When we really understand the process of wealth, however, we realize that if we lost everything tomorrow, we could make it back the next day. There should be no fear in us.

We also saw in the life of Joseph that the blessings of God and success are not predetermined for a chosen few. Just because you were not born rich does not mean that you cannot attain wealth. There is a biblical pattern that we saw with Cain and Abel, with Jacob and Esau, and with Joseph's sons, Manasseh and Ephraim. The blessing does not go to the firstborn, the one in line for it. It goes to the one who is willing to do things God's way. It doesn't matter where you started. If you are willing, the blessing is for you. God looks at the heart.

The process of wealth is really quite simple. It is a matter of investment. God wants us to invest in four areas.

1) Invest in yourself—Sow yourself into salvation and into service in the Kingdom. You reap the harvest of eternal life, forgiveness, grace and righteousness.

2) Invest in the tithe—God asks for a tenth of your income. It is a way of putting God first. When you put God first in your finances, He says that He will rebuke the devourer. He will protect your possessions. It is a kind of insurance policy.

3) Invest in the offering—The offering opens the windows of heaven so that blessing is poured out. The

offering is a measurement of love. You will put your treasure where your heart is.

4) Invest in the earth—God doesn't just pour out money into your backyard. You have to give Him something to bless. This can be business, stock, real estate or whatever. But you have to invest if you want to have increase.

Jesus said that He came to save "that" which was lost, not just "those." He wants to reconcile the whole world to His Kingdom. To fully do that, we have to begin to invest so that the wealth of the world is reclaimed though us.

The process means that we don't jump right into great wealth until we are ready for it. David didn't start out by killing a giant. He started with a bear, then a lion and, finally, he took on Goliath. Do not despise small beginnings. You have to start somewhere. You have to overcome the smaller obstacles before you tackle the bigger ones.

Like David, you must first kill the bear of debt. You must learn not to buy things you don't need with your credit card. Don't go into needless debt. Debt will rob you of the seed you need for investment.

Then you must kill the lion of want. You must curb your desire for things you don't need. Once you have dealt with the bear and the lion, you will be ready to take on the giant of poverty and you will win.

One of the most important things we can learn is to do what we need to do before we do what we want to do. We have to learn to discipline ourselves. We need to learn to make our need tos into want tos and then it becomes easy.

All of success, our ability to make wise choices and to take advantage of opportunities, hinges on what is programmed in our hearts. Wealth is an appropriate reaction to an opportunity. That means that if wealth is in us, we will seize opportunities for wealth without hesitation. If poverty is in us, we will react in poverty and miss the opportunity. What is in us is the controlling factor of what is around us.

We are made up of body, soul and spirit. The body is just dirt and the spirit is born again. It doesn't need anything. It is the soul that needs work.

The soul is made up of the mind, will and emotions. There is also the conscious mind and the unconscious mind. It is in the unconscious mind, the heart, that all of our reactions are programmed. It is out of the heart that the issues of life spring forth. Those reactions are faster than thoughts and faster than feelings. If we want to be successful, we have to program our subconscious to react appropriately to opportunities for wealth. We have to eliminate the wrong programs and replace them with the Word.

That can only be done when the conscious mind begins to take the Word of God in. The conscious mind is the steering part of the mind. It determines what will be planted in the subconscious. It is the gardener, the seed planter. The subconscious is the garden. What we plant in seed, we will do in deed. Ultimately, our failures in the past have been the result of planting wrong seed.

It is only the Word of God that can change what is in us. That is what we have to plant. It is the power of suggestion that plants the seed and gives us the right reactions to circumstances. The Word is filled with suggestions that we can plant in our hearts. If you don't like the harvest, change the seed.

Understanding that the Word is filled with good suggestions, I want to suggest a few things:

> I suggest that by Jesus' stripes, you are healed.
> I suggest that God gives His children the ability to obtain wealth for His Kingdom.
> I suggest that God sent us joy that we might be happy and joy-filled on this earth, no matter what circumstance comes our way.
> I suggest that God gives us peace in the face of our enemies, a peace that passes understanding.
> I suggest that God gives us love in the face of hate.
> I suggest that God gives us life in the face of sickness, disease, trouble and crisis.
> I suggest that He gives us overcoming power that makes us more than conquerors over every situation and over every circumstance that comes our way.

If those suggestions are not programmed into your subconscious, you need to do some reprogramming. Start planting the seed of too much and that is what you will have—too much.

SALVATION PRAYER

Throughout this book, I have spoken of God's desire for you to be blessed, happy and healthy. None of that means anything, however, if you haven't taken the first step. You need to make Jesus your Lord and Savior.

It is easy to do that. The Bible says that if you believe in your heart and confess with your mouth, then you will be saved. It is a matter of faith. If you want to have that relationship with Jesus now, just pray this short prayer.

Dear heavenly Father,
forgive me for my sin.
Come into my heart.
Jesus, be my Lord and my Savior.
Thank You for giving me
new life in You.
In Jesus' name,
Amen.

Congratulations! You have made the very best decision you have ever made or ever will make. Now you are saved. You are forgiven and you are on your way to heaven. The next step is to grow in this new relationship with God. The best way to do that is to read your Bible every day so that God can speak to you through it, and get involved in a good church so that you can have support and fellowship of other believers.

Now that you are saved, we would love to hear from you! Please call us at (480) 964-4463 so that we can come into agreement with you and bless you with a free Bible.

More Books By The Andersons

DRS. C. THOMAS & MAUREEN ANDERSON
Marriage Beyond the Dream
Health God's Way

DR. C. THOMAS ANDERSON
Becoming a Millionaire God's Way
Will the Real America Please Stand Up?
Get the Hell Out of the Church
Wisdom Wins Volumes I and II
Test Me...Signed God

DR. MAUREEN ANDERSON
Releasing the Miraculous Through Fasting with Prayer
Toxic Emotions
Damaged DNA
Making Impossibilities Possible
Open the Door to Your Miracle (Small Paperback and Spiral Bound)
Confession of God's Word (Leather)

BOOKS IN PROGRESS
Intelligence by Design, Power of the Hebrew Alphabet
7 Creation Laws to Live By
20 Power Principles
33 Chapters Through the Cross

CLASS DISCUSSION

INTRODUCTION

1. What picture does the Garden of Eden provide for us? (p.2)
2. What is the historic symbolism of a river? (p.4)
3. What is the significance of the indication that the four rivers were more than just branches? (p.4)
4. Discuss the meaning of the four rivers' names. (p.4)
5. How do these four rivers represent the scope of the Gospel? (p.5)
6. What do we declare when we preach the Gospel? (p.5)
7. What do we need to understand about money before we have it? (p.6)
8. Why should we seek prosperity? (p.7)
9. How did Jesus tell us to keep our priorities right? (p.8)
10. Discuss work, toil, the curse on the ground, and breaking that curse. (p.8-9)
11. Explain I Timothy 6:10. (p.9)
12. Discuss: "Money is neither good nor bad." (p.10)
13. How do we avoid straying from the faith because of greed? (p.10)
14. There is nothing wrong with having great wealth as long as your trust is where? (p.10)
15. Discuss: "[G]reed is not limited to just rich people." (p.11)
16. What happens to people who hold on to more wealth than is right (Proverbs 11:24)? (p.11-12)

Homework: Before reading Chapter 1, re-read Genesis 2:8-14, Psalm 122:8-9, Matthew 6:33, and I Timothy 6:17

CHAPTER 1

1. Research definitions for the following – capitalism, socialism, communism.
2. What inhibits capitalism? (p.15)
3. How can our attitude toward accountability affect our relationship with government and thus our opportunities? (p.17)
4. What did America learn about socialism? (p.17-18)

Note: p. 21 – The ACLU is the American Civil Liberties Union, a group that attempts to protect Americans when their civil liberties are threatened. It has grown to a large group that lobbies congress and has affected interpretation of the U.S. Constitution.

Note: p. 24 – Please understand that it is not necessary to move to America to enjoy the financial blessings of God! God can bless you right where you are and use you to affect change. You can change an entire nation – Joseph did!

Homework: Before reading Chapter 2, read Luke 2:52.

CHAPTER 2

1. Any religion that steals your freedom of choice or responsibility is a form of what? (p.26)
2. How does one give up his freedom of choice? (p.26)
3. What happens when you constantly blame God or others? (p.26)
4. What is the difference between being educated and being an intellectual? (p.27)
5. Why do you need to develop the ability to learn information you don't really care to learn? (p.28)
6. Did you try the exercise on page 31 without looking at the answer on page 32? What was the result?
7. What is the difference between knowing Scripture versus understanding and applying it? (p.34)
8. What example does Jesus give us in Luke 2:52 regarding the type of education we should pursue and the level of maturity we should aspire to attain? (p.35)
9. Why do you need to involve others in your plan in the problem solving process? (p.36)
10. Whose responsibility is it to train children? What does that training really include? (p. 37-39)
11. Being educated means learning what three things? (p.40)
12. What does it mean to think or get outside the box? (p.32-40)

Homework: Before reading Chapter 3, read Genesis 12:1-3, Philippians 3:14, Genesis 1: 27-28 and Malachi 3:10-11

CHAPTER 3

1. Why is your choice so important? (p.44)
2. Discuss the significance of God's instruction to Abram to "Get out." (p.44)
3. What are the financial characteristics of the "wilderness"? (p.45-46)
4. What will happen if you stay in your financial wilderness? (p.46)
5. Explain God's instruction to Abram regarding family and his father's house. (p.46-48)
6. Define "great nation" as used in God's promise to Abram. (p.48)
7. Explain the meanings of the words *bless*, *blessing*, and *blessed*. (p.48-49)
8. Discuss the following: "The way of the world is the love of money; the way of the Kingdom of God is money for the love of people." (p. 49-50)
9. What keeps people motivated? (p.50)
10. Discuss the process of being fruitful and multiplying in order to take dominion. (p.51)
11. Review the ideas of tithe, offering, and seed as discussed in Malachi 3:10-11. (p.53)
12. How does a seed become an asset that pays a dividend? (p.54)
13. When does the Word work? (p.55)
14. Why did God repeat His will concerning being fruitful and multiplying (Genesis 9:1, 28:3)? (p.55)
15. What removes any excuse for us not fulfilling our purpose to multiply? (p.55)
16. Compare and contrast the concepts of "equal opportunity" and "fairness." (p.56-58)
17. What do you have to do to stop being poor? (p.58, 60)
18. Explain: "True education actually creates inequality." (p.60)
19. Write a personal response to the sentence at the end of Chapter 3: "The question is not how much you are given to start with, but what are you doing with what you have?"

Homework: Before reading Chapter 4, read Matthew 10:16 and 2 Corinthians 5:17-18.

CHAPTER 4

1. What is the meaning of the word "send" in Matthew 10:16? (p.63)
2. Discuss the points of sheep and wolves in Matthew 10:16. (p. 62, 64-65)
3. Explain the meaning of the phrase "wise as serpents." (p.66)
4. Explain the meaning of the phrase "harmless as doves." (p.68)
5. Explain the use of the word "lambs" versus "sheep" in Luke 10:3. (p.69)
6. What is our part in the "ministry of reconciliation"(2 Corinthians 5:18)? (p.70)
7. How do you identify and treat wolves who make their way into the church? (p.72)

Homework: Before reading Chapter 5, read Proverbs 3:19-20, Genesis chapters 37 and 39-47 (the story of Joseph).

CHAPTER 5

1. In the process of gaining knowledge, understanding, and wisdom, what does knowledge of the Word provide? (p.74)
2. Why aren't knowledge and understanding enough? (p.74)
3. How is this process of knowledge, understanding, and wisdom completed in the context of financial wealth? (p.74)
4. What is the greatest success stopper and why? (p.75)
5. What kind of person does God need in order to change the world? (p.76)
6. Expound on the statement: "Dreams are critical to success." (p.78)
7. Answer the questions on page 80 and write a personal prayer of commitment.

Homework: Before reading Chapter 6, read Mark 4:3-8, 14-20

CHAPTER 6

1. How does operating under the law affect your ability to receive God's promises? (p.83)
2. What is usually the first thing that happens when God gives you a dream? (p.84)
3. How did Jesus answer the devil in Mark 4 and what does this tell you? (p.84-85)
4. What happens to people when they are excited about a dream but have no root in the Word? (p.85)
5. How should we respond when we run into obstacles? (p.85)
6. What "thorns" distract people from producing? (p.85-86)
7. What is "the deceitfulness of riches" and how do we fight it? (p.86)
8. What is God's way of rising to success? (p.86)
9. Explain the danger of comfort. (p.87)
10. How did Joseph show he had character and what do we need to do to develop it in our lives? (p.89)
11. Discuss two ways to get and stay motivated. Why is moving forward so important? (p.89-90)

Homework: Before reading Chapter 7, read Matthew 6:24-33, I Corinthians 1:26-28, and Genesis 48:1-19

CHAPTER 7

1. Discuss the relationship between fear and security. (p.91)
2. Compare and contrast your relationship with wealth as one who lives in fear or one who lives in faith. (p.92)
3. What is God's plan for your life in simplest form? (p.92)
4. How is your service to God related to your money working for you? (p.92)
5. Discuss the effects of worry. (p.93)
6. What is the remedy to worry Jesus gives us in Matthew 6:33? (p.94)
7. Explain the phrase "Seek first the Kingdom of God" (Matthew 6:33). (p.94)
8. Write a personal response to the statement: "There is no security outside of the knowledge of Christ."
9. How do the three quotes at the bottom of page 97 encourage you? Are there ideas or dreams you have conceived? Do you believe?
10. What is the lesson of Israel, Ephraim, and Manasseh in Genesis 48? (p.100)
11. Who does God respond to? (p.101)
12. Of what does the world's system try to convince you and what does God want to do in contrast? (p.101)
13. What is the secret of wealth that Joseph applied? (p.103)
14. Elaborate on the groups of people described and God's will concerning them in I Corinthians 1:26-28. (p104)

Homework: Before reading Chapter 8, read John 3:16, John 12:24, Genesis 8:22, and 2 Corinthians 9:6-7

CHAPTER 8

1. What are some things that torment people in the world so they can't enjoy their wealth? (p.105)
2. How do we enjoy our prosperity with joy, peace, health, and without worry? (p. 105)
3. Is the principle of investment from the world or from God? Use scripture to support your answer. (p.105-107)
4. Name the four basic investments God requires of us and briefly describe each one. (p.107-113)
5. Explain the dangers of withholding in any of the four areas of investment. (p.113-114)
6. How should our response to the Word be like that of Zacchaeus? (p.116)
7. Explain the significance of the words "that which was lost" in Luke 19:10. (p.116)

Homework: Before reading Chapter 9, read I Samuel 17:34-36

CHAPTER 9

1. What is the process of growth and development that leads to success? (p.119)
2. What are the three giants of finance? (p.119)
3. Write a personal response to Dr. Anderson's statement and question on page 120. Is there someone you admire who fits this quote? *"You determine the caliber of a person by the amount of opposition that it takes to discourage him, but the size of the obstacle or the amount of opposition that it takes to stop him. What does it take to stop you? You need to evaluate that and then change it. There will be some opposition to your dreams. You have to overcome it."*
4. What is the lesson we learn from David's past victories before he took on Goliath? (p.121-122)
5. Explain what debt is. (p.124)
6. What can you do to defeat debt and invest? (p.125)
7. Describe the "Lion of Want." (p.126)
8. You can learn the world's system and beat it, but what do you have to do first? (p.127)
9. What is the significance of David picking up five stones when he only needed one shot to kill Goliath? (p.127)

Homework: Before reading Chapter 10, read Genesis 3:6 and Matthew 26:38-39.

CHAPTER 10

1. If you want to be successful, what must you begin doing? (p.131, 133)
2. Explain the process of desire, passion, motivation and action. (p.132)
3. Discuss training, habits, and "want tos" versus "need tos." (p.134-135)
4. How do you change your need tos into want tos? (p.138-139)

Homework: Before reading Chapter 11, read Proverbs 23:7

CHAPTER 11

1. Discuss the two statements on page 141: "Wealth is an appropriate reaction to an opportunity," and "What is in us is the controlling factor of what is around us."
2. Do you agree with Dr. Anderson's statement that "what is in us is the controlling factor that creates our circumstances"? Why or why not?
3. What idea does Dr. Anderson propose is a small change that would yield big results? (p.142)
4. Discuss the wisdom in "despise not small beginnings" (Zechariah 4:10). (p.143)
5. List the seven things we learn from starting small and briefly describe each one. (p.143-147)
6. Write out the mathematical calculations to show the 30-day example of multiplication on pages 147-148.
7. Discuss the idea of the "gatekeeper" from Proverbs 23:7. (p.149)
8. Discuss how the automatic reactions produced in the subconscious affect wealth. (p.149-152).

Homework: Before reading Chapter 12, read Hebrews 4:12, Hebrews 10:16, and Jeremiah 17:10

CHAPTER 12

1. How can a wrong pattern programmed in your subconscious affect your ability to achieve wealth? (p.154)
2. Why can't you just learn a Bible verse in your conscious mind to produce an appropriate reaction to an opportunity for wealth? (p.154)
3. How do you change your subconscious? (p.154-155)
4. What is the difference in changing your heart and changing your mind? (p.156)
5. Why are we instructed to search our innermost heart? (p.157)
6. How does Jeremiah 17:10 relate to the production of wealth? (p.157-158)
7. Summarize Proverbs 3:3 and Hebrews 10:16. (p.158-159)
8. What are two ways to keep the subconscious programmed positively? (p.161)
9. What is the last line of defense? (p.162)

Homework: Before reading Chapter 13, read 2 Corinthians 10:3-5 and Philippians 4:8

CHAPTER 13

1. What effects do your thoughts, feelings and belief system have on your mind, body and circumstances? (p.167)
2. What happens to fear or doubt when your conscious can trust your subconscious to react appropriately in any given situation? (p.167)
3. Why does the subconscious need to relate directly to the spirit? (p.169)
4. Who actually does the work on the inside of us and why? (p.169)
5. Explain the process of turning thoughts into seed. (p.170)
6. How do we insure that we are constantly planting the right seed? (p.171)
7. What is a stronghold and how do we get rid of it? What happens as you begin to control your thoughts? (p.172-173)

Homework: Before reading Chapter 14, read James 1:14-15, 22-24 and Philippians 3:13

CHAPTER 14

1. Describe the process from suggestion to action. (p.176)
2. Where is the only place you should submit your will and why? (p.177-178)
3. What is the danger in dabbling in various forms of fortune telling? (p.179)
4. Why does Dr. Anderson warn us to "be careful what you allow in the subconscious? (p.180)
5. What is the difference between "doing" and "hearing" the Word? (p.182)
6. How do you overcome circumstances that have been buried in your subconscious? (p.182-183)
7. How does faith operate? What should you do if you don't have the right response to what the Word has for you? (p.183)

CONCLUSION

1. What is God's purpose, and our motivation, for seeking prosperity and what should we be seeking first? (p.185)
2. What are the roles of knowledge, understanding, and wisdom in the process of learning how to think? (p.186)
3. What are some choices we must make like Abraham, to be blessed and bless others? (p.186)
4. What is the greatest enemy we face and why do we seek it? (p.187-188)
5. What is the lesson in the stories of Cain and Abel, Jacob and Esau, and Manasseh and Ephraim? (p.188)
6. What are the four areas of investment and why does God want you to invest in them? (p.188-189)
7. Discuss: "Do not despise small beginnings." (p.189)
8. What is one of the most important things we need to learn in acquiring wealth God's way? (p.189-190)
9. Summarize the role of the subconscious mind in the process of acquiring "too much." (p190-191)
10. What is the only thing that can truly change us? (p.191)

The Harrison House Vision

Proclaiming the truth and the power

Of the Gospel of Jesus Christ

With excellence;

Challenging Christians to

Live victoriously,

Grow spiritually,

Know God intimately.

ABOUT THE AUTHOR

Dr. C. Thomas Anderson is senior pastor and founder of The Living Word Bible Church in Mesa, Arizona. With 30 years of experience in ministering the Gospel, he continues to travel the world leaving a mark that can never be erased. Dr. Tom Anderson is known worldwide for an easy-going teaching style and for the practical, positive, life-changing information that he presents. He has been married over 40 years to his wife, Maureen and they are the proud parents of two boys and the grandparents of nine.

Printed in Great Britain
by Amazon

78863021R00129